Weak enough
for God to use

Dennis Lennon

G000253628

Scripture Union

Scripture Union, 207–209 Queensway, Bletchley, MK2 2EB, England.

© Dennis Lennon 1999

First published 1999

ISBN 1 85999 290 0

All rights reserved. No part of this publication may be reproduced, stored in a retrieval system, or transmitted, in any form or by any means, electronic, mechanical, photocopying, recording or otherwise, without the prior permission of Scripture Union.

The right of Dennis Lennon to be identified as author of this work has been asserted by him in accordance with the Copyright, Designs and Patents Act 1988.

Unless otherwise attributed, scriptures quoted are from the Holy Bible, New International Version. Copyright © 1973, 1978, 1984 by International Bible Society. Anglicisation copyright © 1979, 1984, 1989. Used by permission of Hodder and Stoughton Limited.

British Library Cataloguing-in-Publication Data
A catalogue record for this book is available from the British Library.

Cover design by ie Design.
Cover illustration by Ben Ecclestone.
Printed and bound in Great Britain by Cox & Wyman, Reading, Berkshire.

CONTENTS

	Acknowledgements	4
	Preface	7
1	The God of small things	9
2	Safely out of our depth	17
3	A poor man's arithmetic	25
4	Hiddenness	37
5	Misphat	43
6	The child, the clown and the Pied Piper	51
7	'The soft, barely audible sound of almost breathing'	59
8	Love with a shaken mind	67
9	By way of exchanged life	75
10	Before work	83
11	Slow gold	91
12	The humiliated fool	101
13	Jars, thorns and power	109
14	To know the fellowship of his sufferings	121
15	Orchestrations	131
16	Finally yourself	145

ACKNOWLEDGEMENTS

Chapter 1, The God of small things
1   'The kingly crown', Solomon Ibn Gabriol (medieval Hebrew poet).

2   S K Okazaki, The Gospel and our Culture, vol 7, 1/2.

Chapter 2, Safely out of our depth
1   Austin Farrer, Said or Sung, The Faith Press, 1964, p174. An
     Oxford theologian, Farrer was a remarkable preacher and a
     personal friend of C S Lewis.

Chapter 3, A poor man's arithmetic
1   Farrer, Said or Sung, p18.

2   'The deer's cry', Kuno Myer's translation of St Patrick's hymn.
     This version is found in David Adam, The Cry of the Deer,
     Triangle/SPCK, 1994.

3   David Sherwin, A Prayer-Evangelism Strategy, Grove Books
     Limited, May 1994, p14.

Chapter 4, Hiddenness
1   Emily Dickinson (1830–1886), 'Poem 288'. Reprinted by
     permission of the publishers and the Trustees of Amherst
     College, from THE POEMS OF EMILY DICKINSON, Thomas H
     Johnson, ed, Cambridge, Mass: The Belknap Press of Harvard
     University Press, copyright © 1951, 1955, 1979, 1983 by the
     President and Fellows of Harvard College.

2   Sherwin, Strategy, pp6–7.

Chapter 5, Misphat
1   Emilie Schindler, Where Light and Shadow Meet, Norton, p106.

Chapter 6, The child, the clown and the Pied Piper
1   Hudson Taylor's Choice Sayings, Morgan and Scott, p38.

2   Melba Maggay, Transforming Society, Regnum Lynx, 1994, p90.

3   John Finney, Recovering the Past, Darton Longman and Todd, 1996, p71.

4   An address given by Gary Mason in Maynooth, 1997.

Chapter 7, 'The soft, barely audible sound of almost breathing'

1   Lawrence Kushner, The Book of Words, Jewish Lights Publishing, 1993, p27.

2   Gerard Manley Hopkins (1844–1889), 'Pied beauty', The Poems, Oxford Paperbacks, 1967.

Chapter 8, Love with a shaken mind

1   Elie Wiesel, Souls on Fire, Penguin Books, 1986. This compilation copyright © Elie Wiesel 1972.

2   Brenda Holton, The Overseas Missionary Fellowship in Thailand.

3   Kosuke Koyama, Three Mile an Hour God, SCM Press, 1979, p54.

4   T S Eliot, Choruses from 'The Rock', Collected Poems, Faber, 1974, p163.

5   The Essential G K Chesterton, Oxford Unversity Press, 1987, p46.

Chapter 9, By way of exchanged life

1   This definition is found in Credo by Hans Urs von Balthasar, T&T Clark, 1990, p21.

2   John le Carré, The Honourable Schoolboy, Pan, 1997, p446.

3   Dom Helder Camara, fromThe Isaiah Vision: Ecumenical strategy for congregational evangelism by Raymond Fung, WCC Publications, 1992, p36.

4   Fung, Isaiah, pp28–29,37.

Chapter 10, Before work

1   Balthasar, The Grain of Wheat - Aphorisms, Ignatius Press, 1995, p109.

2   Karl Barth, from Meditations by L Boros, Search Press, 1974, p44.

3   Balthasar, Aphorisms, p92.

Chapter 11, Slow gold

1   Elsa Tamez, from On Job: God talk and the suffering of the innocent by Gustavo Gutierrez, Orbis Books, Maryknoll, New York, USA, 1989.

2   Reprinted from The Message of the Psalms by Walter

Brueggemann, copyright © 1984 Augsburg Publishing House. Used by permission of Augsburg Fortress (US).

3   Hopkins, from his 'Sermons', Poems, p263.

4   George Macdonald - an Anthology, C S Lewis (ed), Geoffrey Bles, an imprint of HarperCollins Publishers.

5   Balthasar, from Hans Urs Von Balthasar by John O'Donnell, Geoffrey Chapman, 1992, p72.

Chapter 12, The humiliated fool

1   Gregory Petrov, 'The Akathist of Thanksgiving', English translation by Mother Thekla, Chester Music Ltd.

2   Bishop Casaldaliga, from We Drink from Our Own Wells by Gustavo Gutierrez, SCM 1984, p118.

3   Martin Hengel, Crucifixion, Fortress Press (US), 1978, p90.

4   Daniel Hardy and David Ford, 'Jubilate' taken from Theology in Praise by Hardy and Ford, published and copyright 1984 by Darton, Longman and Todd Ltd, p106.

5   Lesslie Newbigin, Mission in Christ's Way, copyright © WCC Publications, 1987.

Chapter 13, Jars, thorns and power

1   Balthasar, Aphorisms, p127.

Chapter 15, Orchestrations

1   George Herbert (1593–1633), 'Obedience', The Complete English Poems, Penguin, 1991.

2   Manna Newsletter, September 1998.

3   Kushner, God was in this place, Jewish Lights Publishing, 1993, p117.

Chapter 16, Finally yourself

1   Farrer, A Celebration of Faith, reproduced by permission of Hodder and Stoughton Limited, 1970, p200.

2   Farrer, Celebration, p200.

3   D H Lawrence, 'Things men have made', English Verse 1900–1939, Cambridge University Press, 1971, p81.

4   Fung, Isaiah, p44.

5   Hopkins, 'As kingfishers catch fire', Poems.

PREFACE

'The Lord was looking for someone weak enough to use – and he found me.' Such was James Hudson Taylor's summary of his extraordinary ministry in nineteenth-century China. A startling and very unmodern vision of how we experience God's power, it reflects Hudson Taylor's understanding of the nature of spiritual fruitfulness, an understanding that has been validated time and again since the first forming of God's covenant people at the exodus. Event after event, story after story, person after person bear witness to the paradox of God's strength made perfect in our weakness. Time after time, powerless and excluded human beings are taken up by the Lord and enabled to live lives of extraordinary richness as they fulfil his purposes for the world. Statistics can never encompass the depth and extent, the mystery and the wisdom of what Christ is doing among his frail people.

In this book, we have sought to strike up a conversation between biblical teaching and the lived experience of Christian people. I am most grateful to the many who have kindly sent me accounts of their own dark and testing times, circumstances of 'wit's-end' despair, in which the Lord came to them unexpectedly. I have also heard from congregations which have come through life-out-of-death experiences. Many have described to me their feelings of disorientation as they cast around for fresh ways of understanding what God is up to in their lives, his strange way of manifesting his power. Some are finding it a lonely search.

Where stories are particularly private and personal I have thought it best to change names or to omit them altogether.

Dennis Lennon

Chapter 1

THE GOD OF SMALL THINGS

Any list of 'things that are slow and boring' might include the shipping forecast, paint drying, the sermons of certain preachers, cricket on a damp afternoon and watching a small fire in the outback of the ancient Near East...

Moses knew all about 'slow and boring'. He had been looking after sheep in the wilderness, it seemed, for ever. Here he was, the golden boy banished to the sticks, his glittering Egyptian career wrecked; yesterday's man, rudderless and adrift in circumstances offering no prospects for the future other than this interminable shepherding. His frustration and sense of impotence are pictured by his location that day on 'the far side of the desert', on 'Horeb, the mountain of God' (Exod 3:1).

To the Hebrew imagination, the desert symbolised both the physical wilderness and its spiritual counterpart; it was the place of demons and the night-hag, the vampire and the deadly snake, a metaphor for personal desolation. Theologically speaking, the wilderness is the place of non-being and chaos. The root meaning of 'Horeb' is 'aridity' and 'ruin'. Yet this bare peak is also called 'the mountain of God'.

It started as just another ordinary working day: nothing special – not a high, holy day, not a festival; Moses was not on a pilgrimage. An average ordinary day, like most of our days throughout the year. Then he noticed a bush on fire. Nothing sensational about that – spontaneous combustion amongst tinder-dry wood in that area would not be uncommon. Except that this fire burned on and on and on...

> Moses saw that though the bush was on fire it did not burn up. So Moses thought, 'I will go over and see this strange sight – why the bush does not burn up.'
>
> *(Exodus 3:2-3)*

We commonly interpret the event as a miracle by which God waved to Moses and called him over. Yet it fails to explain why God – who could make the sun stand still, split open the sea and turn Balaam's ass into a philosophical chatterbox – would use something as unremarkable as a burning bush to get Moses' attention. Given his depressing circumstances, and knowing what tremendous plans God had for the man, surely Moses' greatest need at that moment was for a far more spectacular act of empowerment, something that would spark in him a new sense of purpose. The burning bush was a miracle, but only just; a miracle almost buried within the unmiraculous; a miracle seen only by those who will pay attention. It was a miracle, but primarily it was a test.

Clothed in the ordinary

Was Moses open enough to God's world? Was he inquisitive enough, focused enough, to pay attention to something for six minutes without falling asleep? Not too much to ask, you may say.

The people who produce television commercials, who have vast amounts riding on their ability to guess our attention span, reckon our top limit today is about one minute. Most of us would probably have glanced at the burning bush and changed channels to find something more entertaining. We would have failed the test.

How long did Moses watch the blaze before he realised that there was something rather strange going on here? God wanted to know this man's powers of awareness, his ability to intuit divine activity within ordinary life. Did Moses have enough humility to bother to look for God at work in the everyday?

We are inclined to look over the head of the commonplace, searching for divine fireworks in the night sky. But the Creator loves his creation and honours it by coming to us clothed in its familiar ordinariness. When God finally answered Job (Job 38–42), he allowed creation in all its variety to speak on his behalf. When, in Jesus, he came into the world for our salvation, he took upon himself that most humble of human forms, a baby. When Jesus taught eternal things, he did so by means of everyday commonplace things (see Matt 13). He promised to meet us in the water of baptism, and in bread and wine.

Poet George Herbert prayed, 'Lord, be a standing majesty in the midst of us.' At moments of disclosure, when we sense that the Lord is indeed here in the midst of everyday events, we feel our senses stretched beyond ordinary use. In Moses' case, God first aroused his curiosity and fired his imagination – and only then spoke a word. Believers in the past called the senses 'the talismans of the Lord', each one taking some part in our encounters with him:

> Who can know the secret of your accomplishments, when
> you made for the body the means of your work?
> You gave him eyes to see your signs,
> Ears, to hear your wonders,
> Mind, to grasp some part of your mystery,
> Mouth, to tell your praise,

> Tongue, to relate your mighty deeds to every corner,
> As I do today, I tell according to the shortness of my
>   tongue, one tiny part of your greatness.
>
> *(Solomon Ibn Gabriol)*[1]

The burning bush demonstrates the Lord's freedom to choose how he makes himself known to us. Fire is not God nor is it the glory of God; but, in this symbolic and sacramental world, fire (like all aspects of the created order) is transparent to God. The writer of the book of Esdras puts it beautifully: 'Your glory passed through the four gates of fire and earthquake and wind and ice, to give the law to the descendants of Jacob' (2 Esdras 3:19). God came to Moses through the gate of the burning bush; and then God spoke.

For us, the question is why our own encounters with God are so piecemeal and elusive. He is the great God, who loves and honours small things. Our daily lives are filled with small things, which should give the Lord plenty of scope to come to us. Where is the obstacle?

'Mostly asleep, most of the time'

The greatest of all illusions is the illusion of familiarity. Familiarity is the death of expectancy, of respect, of awe and wonder. Jesus suffered by it: 'Nazareth! Can anything good come from there?' (John 1:46). But, like Moses as he looked into the flames, we need to acquire a new appreciation that created things can be a gate for the Lord; we need to catch 'the sacrament of the present moment' as God comes to us under cover of ordinary and unremarkable phenomena. 'Our perennial spiritual and psychological task is to learn to look at things familiar until they become unfamiliar again' (G K Chesterton). In Jesus' more homely words, we must 'become like a child' (Matt 18:2–4).

Children are not yet blunted and dulled by custom. They are not yet under the gloomy tyranny of habit. Everything strikes the young imagination as new. However, seventeenth-century Christian mystic Thomas Traherne defined the problem for us: 'Were we to see [the world] only once, that first appearance would amaze us. But being seen daily, we observe it not'. In fact, most of us are mostly asleep most of the time, oblivious of the Lord's approaches. We must awaken our dozing minds from the lethargy of custom. Real life is lived in awareness of the mystery of God. At any moment, on any spot, we can become aware that 'the place where [we] are standing is holy ground' (Exod 3:5). This was the first principle God established with Moses at the start of his epic ministry.

Something very similar happened to that complex man, Jacob, when he camped out one night, in the middle of nowhere, and by next morning realised, 'Surely the Lord is in this place, and I was not aware of it ... How awesome is this place! This is none other than the house of God; this is the gate of heaven' (Gen 28:16–17).

The question is not whether God will come to us, but whether we will discern him as he signals to us from within the ordinary business of our daily lives. 'As a man is, so he sees. As the eye is formed, such are its powers' (William Blake). Most of us will admit that we are not alert to, aware of or attuned to God's presence in the midst of life. Deadly familiarity has rendered the humdrum the last place where we would look for his activity. Consequently, we are forever taking our eye off the present moment to seek out more glamorous situations elsewhere: 'Can anything good come out of my circumstances?'

Concentration, the ability to attend intensely to something for any length of time, is a real problem. We go through life with a metaphorical 'TV channel selector' in our brain, flicking between things of fleeting interest. Thus, in many of our church services, more and more effort and ingenuity are expended in attempts to hold people's attention for a few minutes longer. It is not difficult to see from where the mischief is coming. The noise, the static, the wall-to-wall muzak of the marketplace drowns out God's voice. Our imaginations and desires are under constant bombardment from the world around us. Our inner life becomes fragmented, atomised, addicted to stimuli, distracted, restless, to the extent that we may reach a state of nervous exhaustion.

'You, Lord, were within me, but I was in the world outside myself ... you were with me, but I was not with you' (Augustine). All the lights are on, but we are not at home. In that state of inner life (if indeed it can be said that such a person has an inner life) we walk on, oblivious to the Lord's attempts to attract our attention and call us over. The bush is blazing but we plod on, head down, unaware, complaining that the Lord's presence is so elusive.

This is why it is said:
  'Wake up, O sleeper,
    rise from the dead,
  and Christ will shine on you.'
        (Ephesians 5:14)

Discern the Lord in 'wit's-end' situations
It was while he was going nowhere in the back of beyond that Moses had his life-changing encounter with God. Perhaps we become more open to the Holy Spirit when we are at our wit's end.

When coal-mine closures hit the mining village of Armthorpe in South Yorkshire, the small local congregation were not sure what they could do to indicate their solidarity with the families of the men thrown out of work. So they went to the pit gates to pray. Where was God in the all too familiar experience of unemployment? And something happened – as if that symbolic act sent out a signal to the community about God's love for people. The congregation has since grown rapidly, and continues to grow. They have planted another church, operate a drop-in centre five mornings a week and a toy library, and pay for the Citizens Advice Bureau to be present in the village every Wednesday. This despite a senior member of the hierarchy in Sheffield Diocese telling John Barnes, the vicar, not to expect any church growth in South Yorkshire! God can bless his people in the most discouraging circumstances, if only they are alert to his presence.

In the following account, a small, struggling, ageing church becomes aware of the Lord's presence among homeless people in New York:[2]

> The church had only fifty members, mostly elderly (if you were forty, you were part of the youth group), and was struggling to grow. We were surrounded by Catholics, and Orthodox Jews and there were also a number of Muslims, Hindus and Buddhists as well. The neighbourhood was too expensive to live in, but not fancy enough or convenient enough, so people didn't stay. The church had constant financial difficulties so they learned to rent out the church space for anything for money. But this church, which struggled to survive, operated a homeless shelter. During the winter months, four days a week, we picked up fifteen men from a centre in Southern Queens. We brought them to our fellowship hall and served them supper. After eating and fellowship with them, we slept in the same premises with them. In the morning we served them breakfast and sent

them to the centre with a lunch.

The church building was very small, smaller than any of the churches I've seen outside of the city. All of the work was done by volunteers from our church and by neighbours and friends of the church. The city reimbursed the church for heat and electricity, provided the beds and linens so that the cost to the church was relatively low, but it was a great effort to make for such a small church. They have been providing this shelter for seven years now.

This is a small mission work that they could do for the world. They do as much as they can as a small, struggling church. But, interestingly, by doing this work of healing, they are not only enriching society, but they also enrich their own identity. They transform themselves from a small, struggling church to an inviting, open church. They transform themselves from a needy church to a church that works for the needy. They transform themselves from a passive, surviving church to an active agent of God.

If this church did not have this homeless shelter, I think it might have been dead a long time ago. I am not sure if they are conscious of that, but the vision of mission to the needy gives them a reason for existence. A reason to be God's people. A reason to be a 'light to the nations'.

(S K Okazaki)

The Lord appears in the flames of a burning bush, the despair of unemployment and the misery of homelessness. In each case, he finds people who are open to him and weak enough to use. Even arid, barren Horeb can become 'the mountain of God'.

Chapter 2

SAFELY OUT OF OUR DEPTH

A man set the greatest task of his life at the age of eighty will understand what it is to be nervous about doing the will of God. Moses speaks for all who are out of their depth when it comes to God's call. God calls us to a life of holiness and love, and to particular acts of ministry, and we cannot cope. But we never will know his power while we stay within the limits of our own powers and competence, splashing about in the shallows of the familiar. Experience confirms over and over that when we face up to our inability to handle God's call, we receive new empowerment in the Holy Spirit.

We do not have because we do not ask, and we do not ask because we do not feel any great need to ask while we manage quite nicely within the comfort zone of our small spiritual ambitions. But once we are kicked into the light, out of our complacency, we find ourselves out of our depth, like Moses.

Moses was in his eighties when God called him to the work of leading the exodus (Exod 7:7). A case for Age Concern? But there is no ageism in the kingdom of God. Believers have always known the secret of staying young, the paradox of keeping oneself by giving oneself away (John 12:24–26).

The person who reaches out for what lies ahead of him is always becoming younger than himself ... God's commandments are to be fulfilled with an inexhaustible yearning that is ever making haste.

(Basil the Great, fourth century)

Arthritic joints, yes, but what does that matter if there is fire in the mind? There is no place in this vision of growing older for killing time with interminable golf and gardening.

I was privileged to work with George Harris, a venerable missionary to the Islamic world. He had spent his life engaging with Muslims in North China and South East Asia. He once told me that he had never personally led a Muslim to faith in Jesus Christ. Yet this old man (when I knew him) was unfailingly optimistic, full of love for his Muslim neighbours and happy to play his part in those 'good works which God prepared in advance for him to do'. When his wife died, he was at an age when most of us would be taking a well-earned rest. George astonished us all by taking to the road, seeking out Muslims with whom he could share his knowledge of Jesus Christ, before compulsory retirement sent him home.

Isaiah observed the same renewing processes in those he described as 'the weak and the weary' – God's defeated people, forced to live in an environment of triumphant paganism during Israel's Babylonian captivity.

Even youths grow tired and weary,
    and young men stumble and fall;
but those who hope in the Lord
    will renew their strength.
They will soar on wings like eagles;
    they will run and not grow weary,
    they will walk and not be faint.

(Isaiah 40:30–31)

We too know the depressing effects of the steady drip-drip of a confident culture content to live without God. Capitulation and assimilation to prevailing attitudes seems inevitable. But Isaiah saw astonishing transformations in his exhausted believers 'who hope in the Lord'. They outstrip the best young athletes as they seem to move by laws other than the laws of nature (v 31).

How is it done? The vast cosmetics and fitness industries would kill to know the secret of continuous rejuvenation. But, if told, they would never believe it. The idea that the weak and the weary can transcend the down-drag of life by abandoning themselves in love to the God of love sounds fanatical, suicidal, life-hating nonsense. Self-preservation is the name of their game. Christians, meanwhile, fix their lives on the living Lord and fly like eagles. 'Obedience to gravity is the greatest sin' (Simone Weil).

Think of the enormity of Moses' assignment. Imagine his sense of self-sufficiency melting away as God's words dawned on him. He must lead a huge, demoralised slave-tribe out of the terrible Egyptian brickyards, to embark on an incredible journey into the dangerous unknown. It is difficult to think of a comparable enterprise of such lunatic audacity. Imagine a Jew living comfortably with his family in Switzerland in 1943. One day he drives back into Germany, where he is still wanted on a murder charge, walks into Hitler's HQ and demands the immediate release of all Jews in the concentration camps!

Grace in unlikely places

A wise employer would have appointed a diplomatic genius for the job, someone on good terms with Egypt and Israel, someone with the communications skills to charm the birds out of the trees. Instead God chose Moses, a man on the run for murder and therefore with good reason to keep as far away from Egypt as possible. Moses' privileged upbringing as the protégé of an Egyptian princess set him a world apart from his own oppressed people (Exod 2:1–11). As for 'relevant experience', we look in vain in his CV: plenty of time spent with sheep; little by way of large-scale, creative personnel management. And, taking his self-assessment at face value, he was a dull, uninspiring speaker, 'slow of speech and tongue', hardly one to sway the Israelite masses. To cap it all, Moses simply did not want the job: 'O Lord, please send someone else to do it' (Exod 4:13).

No denomination would ordain a man like Moses. Probably no theological college would admit him for training. No missionary agency would give him a job. His past, his circumstances, his lack of relevant experience, his present attitudes and, finally, sheer common sense are stacked against his selection. He is floundering out of his depth as God's hands close around his life. Yet God gives strength in weakness, life out of death, blessing out of despair. We call this strange way with power, 'grace'. We read Moses' story and recognise within it our own.

I asked a young minister to comment on the growth and blessing he has experienced in a very tough area, where 'tough' comes in the form of massive local indifference to the gospel. I have long admired his work and looked forward to what he would say. His answer opened with these startling words.

The greatest tragedy I have suffered in my time here is the failure of my marriage. I think it would be fairer to say that I failed my marriage and not simply that my marriage failed, as though it were an entirely impersonal thing. My wife left me, taking with her our three children ... the horror of that experience still returns to haunt me regularly ... the growth of the congregation here can be traced roughly to the time when my marriage failed. It was as though the Lord was saying, 'You have lost one family through your own sin, but I am giving you another.'

Then followed a modest, very moving account of the numbers of local people touched by God under his ministry: 'the far side of the desert ... Horeb, the mountain of God' (Exod 3:1).

Sarah had promised to go with others in her church to help another congregation with their house-to-house visiting. Then came the devastating blow of her husband's death. Even so, Sarah felt she ought to keep her promise. She went, feeling in no state of mind for calling on total strangers in their homes in another part of the city. But she was amazed at the number of people she met who were also going through dark times, including recent bereavement. Sarah found herself welcomed by them in that unique bond of a common distress. Without the strain we often feel when we attempt to share our faith with others, particularly when on their ground, Sarah was able to speak of her own experience of Christ's healing presence. Although she does not use the term about herself, Sarah was fulfilling the Christ-role of wounded healer. Her own weakness in her grief, and the vulnerable love which took her out to others, qualified her to speak of the Father's loving care.

Stand out of your own light

God uses powerless and excluded human beings. At the exodus he brought to birth his covenant people, Israel, through a powerless and excluded man. It seems that our weakness allows God to be himself with us. He has scope to move as he works through us in our powerlessness.

Here we must tread carefully to avoid a possible

misunderstanding. It is not that our abilities, gifts, personality or brains are ever a hindrance in the service of God! As a wise writer put it, 'God is no trainer of souls bent on attaining extravagant record performances. He is a lover who wants nothing but great love and who accepts with a smile everything such love invents to offer him. But he declines everything man uses – no matter how subtly – to put on airs before him!' The powers and abilities we possess from God are not the problem, but the vanity and idolatrous self-sufficiency they may induce in us are a very real hindrance. How much of my so-called discipleship is an attempt to put on airs before God? We are too easily bewitched by 'success'. With naïve arrogance, we settle down into the driving seat and take imperious command of the steering wheel. Things which should be done out of love for God and neighbour merely serve to fuel our narcissism.

Illusions are bad for us and usually end in tears. But 'God delights in disillusionment' (Patrick Kavanagh). A healthy practical dependence upon him is a sign that we have become disillusioned about our absurd notions of autonomy. Splendid. Now we are real enough, weak enough, for God to take up and use. Writer Austin Farrer prayed for deliverance from this sticky, clogging self:[1]

> O God, save me from myself, this frivolous self which plays with your creation, this vain self which is clever about your creation, this masterful self which manipulates your creation, this greedy self which exploits your creation, this lazy self which soothes itself with your creation; this self which throws the thick shadow of its own purposes and desires in every direction in which I try to look, so that I cannot see what it is that you, my Lord and God, are showing to me. Teach me to stand out of my own light and let your daylight shine!

What you are – what you might become

The Christian life is like mountaineering: each step is a debate between what you are and what you might become. The thing we fear most is to look ridiculous. Moses was at this point: anyone who has ever feared ridicule if a risky project fails will easily decode his protestations (Exod 3:11–13; 4:1). 'What if I attempt this thing for God and it flops? What if we do make a start and ten miles down the road the whole thing fizzles out?' The sneering 'We told you so' of the critics can have dire consequences. How much potentially great work never sees the light of day, not through lack of resources or because of physical danger, but because of the fear of failure and the ridicule of the know-alls on the touch-line?

A congregation in Edinburgh was preparing to plant a new church. It was a big venture in which some seventy people would leave to form the new congregation. As plans evolved, the nagging question which could not be answered was 'What if this thing goes wrong?' Even the bishop felt he should raise the possibility: 'If this thing fails, you risk losing your people and your money.' Not to mention your credibility, your reputation and your confidence.

In retrospect, it was that fear of looking foolish, of delighting the critics and enemies by their failure, which most troubled the congregation and made some unsure of the wisdom of the experiment. In fact, the Lord has richly blessed both the sent congregation and the mother congregation in ways beyond anyone's expectations. However, nobody could have guaranteed the outcome. It really was a case of being weak enough, scared enough, uncertain enough, nervous enough for God to do something with his dependent people.

Weak enough means wise enough to allow God to enfold our weakness within his power and authority.

23

These rather abstract terms were embodied for Moses in a name that sounds like breathing. But this is for the next chapter...

Chapter 3

A POOR MAN'S ARITHMETIC

We are all insecure, and we each think that this insecurity is our own private, secret problem. But everyone is the same. Experts may tour the chat shows, urging us to take control, to triumph over our feelings of inadequacy, but a course in self-enhancement will not help.

Moses was in crisis. Facing the wrath of a particularly unpleasant Pharaoh, he needed something more than shiny self-esteem. We recognise the smell of fear and hope, danger and opportunity, expectation and paralysis which seize the mind in crisis. It is time he did his sums.

What have faith and calculations to do with each other? Jesus is clear that they belong together. He amused the crowds with stories of local follies, the work of absurdly incompetent planners – a half-finished tower, a farcical attempt to fight a battle. The bottom line is that anyone who decides to take up the work of the kingdom should 'first sit down and estimate the cost' (Luke 14:25–35). Calculation is necessary because real faith operates in the real world. However, sound arithmetic is possible only when done in the penetrating clarity of faith which sees things as they really are. Lazy triumphalism has no place in the promises we make to our Lord.

Aware of the high risk of the exodus, Moses probably worried about his ability to see the job through to the end. Did he have the staying power for 'a long obedience in the same direction'? Those reasonable considerations are one part of the equation: the other part is the resources available to him in God. Before Moses had taken a step along the road to Pharaoh's front door, God settled the question. He clothed his servant in power and authority. As Christians, with our uncertainties and crises of faith on our own exodus walk, we should be intensely interested in these divine resources.

The name
God did not immediately plug Moses into a spiritual power supply of 10,000 volts; instead, he tells him his name. Volts are naked power; a name invites relationship. So, rather than impersonal power, God opts for a personal relationship of love and trust.

Moses asked, 'What is your name?' (Exod 3:13), meaning 'Who are you?' In the culture of the Bible, a person's name was his or her essential reality transposed into a word. When the Pharaohs wanted to break the power of an enemy, they would inscribe that enemy's name onto a pot and smash it. Shattered name equals shattered power.

God replied, Ehyeh-asher-ehyeh, a name which eludes our grasp as it moves in all directions. Our English translation, 'I am who I am', is too static and philosophical. The name dynamically faces the future: 'I will be who I will be'. Writer G A F Knight suggests that we must release 'be' from its static mode into 'become': 'I will become with you'. Thus God is saying, 'I will meet you in each event of your journey, and you will find that I will be whatever I need to be in order to bless you and fulfil my covenant promises to you.' Another scholar renders the name, 'I am there, wherever it may be ... I am really there!' (Vrietzen). The best expositions of Ehyeh-asher-ehyeh are found in experience.

The various crises experienced during the exodus demonstrate the name in creative and redemptive action, which is the only way God reveals himself. The Israelites found themselves dangerously low on water (Exod 17:1–7). God allowed the crisis to develop, waiting for Moses and the people to draw level with him: 'Walk on ... I will stand there before you by the rock at Horeb ... and water will come out of it'. He will meet them with the form of love and power required by that moment. We cannot learn the meaning of his name in the classroom. The name by which God launches his people into the exodus is an invitation to walk with him and to prove him each time in the fires of lived experience.

In the New Testament, the mysterious Ehyeh-asher-ehyeh is elaborated in Christ's self-revelation to the churches: 'I am the Alpha and the Omega ... who is, and who was, and who is to come, the Almighty' (Rev 1:8). As Moses received the name as his power and authority in Egypt, the church receives God's name as her authority for her mission in a hostile and often persecuting world. In 'I am the Alpha and the Omega', the Lord is saying, 'I will be who I will be and not as you want me to be.' He is the God who is 'not yet' – not yet finished with the church, the world or with us personally.

The name reveals God moving faster than light ahead of us, around us, above us, beneath us, always faithful yet always eluding our theories about him, defeating our pagan instincts to pin him down for our own ends. He is dancing circles around the despotic spiritual powers and their political stooges – the Pharaohs, the Caesars and the Hitlers, all the dark powers which batten onto the life of the world. Only the name of the Lord can heal our insecurities and reintegrate our fragmented inner life. The Alpha and the Omega, the First and the Last, means that nothing in our future can take Christ by surprise, nothing is beyond his mastering reach. He has already defeated all the demons we may meet. He is the author of the play, from Act One (the Alpha) to the final curtain (the Omega). The future is already a familiar story to him. We are involved in a drama far beyond the grasp of any of the actors, happy to play our part without any need to argue with the author or change the script or ask for easier lines to say.

Living under the name

In Moses' place we might have hoped for an exodus-blueprint, a copy of God's five-year plan. Instead Moses was given the divine name which is all the plan his people need. To live under this name is to place all life into the hands of the Lover who is the supreme creative artist. There is indeed a plan for our lives, and it unfolds within the relationship of love as we walk on with God. 'God does not push his creatures into existence like ducklings into a pool to sink or swim, and to fend for themselves. He has a plan for them ... his plans are all the good that his love can see for us' (Farrer).[1]

In practical terms, what does it mean to trust in the name of the Lord each day? One inspiring answer to this question comes down to us from the early Celtic church. St Patrick's Hymn deliberately brings every aspect and every inch of existence, personal and cosmic, from the domain of darkness out into the redeeming, protecting and sanctifying love and power of the name. Several stanzas run like this:[2]

I arise today
Through a mighty strength, the invocation of the
    Trinity,
Through belief in the threeness,
Through confession of the oneness
Of the Creator of Creation.

I arise today
Through the strength of Christ's birth with his baptism,
Through the strength of his crucifixion with his burial,
Through the strength of his resurrection with his
    ascension,
Through the strength of his descent for the judgement
    of Doom...

I arise today
Through God's strength to pilot me:
God's might to uphold me,
God's wisdom to guide me,
God's eye to look before me,
God's ear to hear me,
God's word to speak to me,
God's hand to guard me,
God's way to lie before me,
God's shield to protect me,
God's host to save me
From snares of devils,
From temptations of vices,
From everyone who shall wish me ill,
Afar and near,
Alone and in a multitude...

Christ to shield me today
Against poisoning, against burning,
Against drowning, against wounding,
So there comes to me abundance of reward.
Christ with me, Christ before me, Christ behind me,
Christ in me, Christ beneath me, Christ above me,
Christ on my right, Christ on my left,
Christ when I lie down, Christ when I sit down, Christ
    when I arise,
Christ in the heart of every man who thinks of me,

Christ in the mouth of every one who speaks of me,
Christ in the eye of every one who sees me,
Christ in every ear that hears me.

I arise today
Through a mighty strength, the invocation of the
    Trinity,
Through belief in the threeness,
Through confession of the oneness
Of the Creator of Creation.

The name is all-acting, all-caring, all-wisdom, all-love, all-inclusive, all-enfolding of all our weaknesses and our insecurity.

'Now pick up your snake'

God sent Moses right into the presence of Pharaoh, demanding a total exodus for Israel. But first he gave him what he required. His servant would go into the heart of the satanic HQ covered in the wisdom and power of the great 'I will be who I will be' (Exod 4:1–5). Here is the secret of the believer's authority over the power of evil, given in the symbolism of the snake.

From Eden to the book of the Revelation, the snake in various manifestations (appearing, disappearing and reappearing) plagues human experience. In the imagination of the ancient biblical world, the forces of chaos are figured as a reptile, a serpent-dragon, which constantly threatens God's good creation. Ezekiel speaks of Pharaoh as 'a monster in the seas thrashing about in your streams' (Ezek 32:2).

If you must pick up a snake, the only safe way is to grasp it behind its head so that it cannot whip round and bite. Why then did God specifically direct Moses to grab his snake by the tail (Exod 4:4)? Moses' self-

centred reasoning – his 'What if' and 'I cannot' –
measured the project in terms of his own resources.
Yet he had to understand that the exodus is God's act,
done in God's way and in God's power. He must, in
other words, locate the dynamic centre of exodus in
the love, wisdom and power of God: 'Without God we
cannot – without us he will not' (Augustine). Until he
saw this fundamental truth of God's kingdom, Moses
had better keep well away from Egypt.

Yes, Pharaoh is dangerous and he bites. The moment
Moses did that foolish, irrational, unreasonable thing and
picked up the snake by its tail, he realised that he could
master evil in the power of God. By trusting in God when
it seemed utterly absurd and suicidal to do so, Moses
found himself participating in what God does to evil. God
compels evil to serve his good purposes. Pharaoh will bite
and, in so doing, will destroy himself and release Israel.

Later, when Moses obeyed God and went with his
brother Aaron to meet Pharaoh, he saw Aaron's snake
devour Pharaoh's in a reptilian showdown (Exod 7:8–12).
At that moment Moses surely exploded with Jewish hilar-
ity, the laughter of wonder and recognition at God's infinite invention as he turns evil inside out. Thus, by pick-
ing it up by its tail, Moses did with his snake what God
in Christ did to Satan on the cross. There Jesus received
the deadly bite in his own body for our sakes; he drew
the satanic poison into himself; he 'disarmed the powers
and authorities, he made a public spectacle of them, tri-
umphing over them by the cross' (Col 2:15).

In the imagery of the Revelation, the snake as the
Satan-dragon attacks the Saviour and receives on the
cross its fatal wound (see Revelation 12). The creature is
not annihilated but, in its panic and frenzy, lashes out in
its death throes, 'filled with fury, because he knows that
his time is short' (Rev 12:12). Thus the Christian has the

power to pick up evil by the tail! That is, we overcome within Christ's overcoming. The victory has been won – now win the victory in your own life. Even should the Lord send us to do work in the heart of Satan's HQ, we will overcome because we are clothed in his name and in the authority of his cross.

The extraordinary revealed in the ordinary

Everywhere Christians show how the insignificant and insecure few can live in the most fearsome situations and 'handle their snakes in the power of the name'. Consider the extraordinary growth of the church in China during the twenty years of greatest state hostility. Like the church in the New Testament period, the church in China had no power base in society, no authority or prestige, neither the freedom nor the resources for programmes of mission. Yet expansion has been miraculous, or so it seems to us on the outside who cannot exist without our bureaucracies, our seminars and all the paraphernalia of organised Christian life.

For explanation, we must go to the book of Revelation and the stunning vision of a persecuted Christian minority at prayer (Rev 7:9–17). God calls for hush in the cosmic din ('for about half an hour', 8:1) in order to hear the prayer of his people. We glimpse the complete reversal of this world's idea of power. The weak and insignificant few on earth, praying in Christ's name, are in touch with the deepest mysteries of the historical processes. In response, the angel of the Lord hurls the fire of God back onto the earth, the dangerous fires of God's purposes setting the earth ablaze (8:5). Powerless believers, or so the world sees them, are the real arsonists, the true aggressors against the forces of evil. And yet what could be less threatening or less relevant to a high-speed, 'can-do' society than a few ordinary people on their knees?

David Sherwin gives a fascinating description of the congregation at Conisbrough facing all kinds of opposition, within and outside, and 'casting fire on the earth' through a deliberate ministry of prayer:[3]

> There were times of prayer called for specific reasons. One such reason was in response to the action of a cult within the parish. The group was hiring rooms and attracting a lot of interest for the wrong reasons; so we prayed. Within three months of the special prayer meeting, the group had ceased to meet and the place where they were meeting had changed management. The new management would not let such groups use the premises.
>
> More recently, difficulties were being faced where a service was being held on one of our estates. A small, troublesome and sometimes violent group were doing all they could to disrupt the service. In fact, one of our leaders was physically abused. The church called upon the congregation to pray, and a special prayer meeting was set up. Since that night things improved dramatically, even to the point that some of the troublemakers have been to the service.
>
> So that people did not become narrow in their prayers, we introduced a prayer diary. It encouraged people to pray for other people's streets and the church members who lived there. This ran until it had served its purpose, in that some were making their own prayer diaries, whilst others had set up prayer chains which still operate today.

There is no more appalling test than the tragedy of losing a child. A couple lost their baby. They were helped by the hospital chaplain, and joined a local church. Then, a year later, they lost a set of twins in the womb. Yet they are both increasingly committed, and are now leading a youth group. The conviction that those small lives have not been lost, but are sharing in God's life, has been pivotal in helping them to cope with such a tragedy. Their vicar comments on their conversion:

> There can be little doubt why people are attracted to Christ. It is the extraordinary being disclosed and discovered in the ordinary as the life of Jesus glows through events and activities that ordinary folk can both identify with and engage in ... in this way we recover from the futility of imitating our media-age agenda ... and remind others that in the small, local and engaged, the life of God is found.

A 42-year-old mother of two small children writes:

> In December 1996, I hadn't been to church for about twenty-five years. Then I took my five-year-old daughter to the Christmas service at our village church, expecting no more than a good sing and some mince-pies afterwards. A year later, we haven't missed a Sunday, and I count my Christian faith as the most important thing in my life.
>
> The reason why people like me stay away from church is not because it isn't 'accessible' enough, as if we needed some kind of spiritual wheelchair ramp, but because we don't expect to find anything useful there. What we want is God. If I were asked to run an advertising campaign to make the church more 'accessible', I would base it around the slogan, 'Our God can help'. And I would try to make prayer visible. It is the heart of our Christian lives, the breath of the Spirit's life within us, the most important thing we do. Our churches should reek of it, we should carry the scent on our clothes. It is a daily miracle.

These accounts suggest that we enter the power of God's name, and seize evil by the tail, when we come to God with our weakness and insecurity, in prayer – and in praise:

> [Christians] escape the fiend worshipfully. His [the fiend's] might is all locked in God's hand. At this sight I laughed mightily. After this I said, 'I see three things – game, scorn and earnest. I see game – that the fiend is overcome. And I see scorn – that God scorns him and he shall be scorned. And I see earnest – that he is overcome by the passion of our Lord Jesus Christ and by his death that was done full earnestly and with sad travail.'
>
> *(Julian of Norwich)*

Chapter 4

HIDDENNESS

There is a saying: 'The healing of the world is in its nameless saints' (who we take to include all Christ's faithful people). But in a culture of Big Names, Celebrities and Personalities, to be nameless, to be virtually anonymous, is a particularly sharp experience of 'weakness'.

What must a person be to be effective for God? Hidden. The Lord calls and places us around the world, concealed, for the most part, within the life of the world.

> I'm Nobody! Who are you?
> Are you – Nobody – Too?
> Then there's a pair of us?
> Don't tell! They'd advertise – you know!
> How dreary – to be – Somebody!
> How public – like a Frog –
> To tell one's name – the livelong June –
> To an admiring Bog![1]

Emily Dickinson's opinion of fame has a certain wacky appeal, particularly for the reclusive amongst us. But she did not live in a media-soaked culture like our own, in which the indicator of a successful lifestyle is to be 'known'. In this pushy, self-promoting world, to live as unknown implies insignificance. What a paradox – to achieve lasting spiritual significance through anonymity.

The gospel rejects utterly the secular reading of life. A glance at Philippians 2:5–11 will show why. In order to be totally effective as the world's healer, Jesus 'made himself nothing'. If his rightful glory as co-equal with the Father prevented him from penetrating to the disordered roots of the world, then he would strip off that glory. If his due status as Lord of all stopped him from reaching into the depths of our hearts, then he would take 'the very nature of a servant'. Anything short of that penetration to the centre of our condition would mean that full redemption could not happen. He would be treating the symptoms but not healing the cause of our disorders, responding to our defects but not mastering our defection.

Therefore Jesus avoided fame like the plague. He would not trust popularity an inch (see Isaiah 11:3). He resisted strongly every attempt by man or demon to prevent him going all the way to the cross to bring about our healing. He fought the temptation to court celebrity from the first days of his ministry, when Satan offered to manage his campaign for him (the advertising would be sensational, popular appeal guaranteed, Luke 4:5–8). When his mission was booming, 'knowing that they intended to come and make him king by force, [Jesus] withdrew...' (John 6:15). He knew that he would accomplish more as an 'incarnate nobody'.

Spiritual regeneration flows from the centre out. Fame, renown, reputation would bring merely superficial results and keep Jesus from transforming the heart of the world. Out of love for us, he ducked the temptation to be a Big Name so that he could come close to us. Gaining access to the human heart is an essentially hidden process, like that of yeast, seed and salt.

Metaphors of hiddenness

Jesus compared the life of God's kingdom (ie the way the King works) with these hidden processes of germination (seed, Matt 13:31–32), fermentation (yeast, v 33) and seasoning (salt, 5:13). His people participate in that powerful obscurity when they too live as seed, yeast and salt. Each in itself is quite ordinary, insignificant (try finding a seed once you have dropped one on the floor), small, unremarkable, cheap. But use each according to its nature – bury the seed in the ground, immerse the yeast in the flour and water, sprinkle the salt into the food as it cooks – and transformation follows.

In each case, the effect is out of all proportion to its size or quantity. In each case, the transformation occurs only when the agent of transformation (the seed, the yeast, the salt) 'loses' itself and quite literally disappears, is dissolved in and dispersed throughout the surrounding mass. So it was with Jesus, and so it is with his people, his countless 'nameless saints', who are far too busy exerting their hidden spiritual influence where God has placed each one, to bother with the irrelevant considerations of fame and fortune. It usually takes a catastrophe, like an earthquake or a civil war, to reveal them in the unlikeliest places. The world's media fly in, politicians learn to pronounce new place names, and there on our screens we catch a glimpse of Christians who have been serving the local population for years.

In Thailand, a number of women are coming to the end of their working lives. Each has clocked up over thirty years of service, starting and running leprosy clinics, teaching literacy, translating the scriptures into dialect Malay, communicating the gospel, and caring daily for small groups of converted leprosy sufferers in an Islamic society. These women have knowingly passed up the usual opportunities for marriage and family. Two of their number were kidnapped while running a clinic, and were later murdered. They have seen no great spiritual awakenings or revivals – if anything, Islamic fundamentalism has intensified. But leprosy is now largely under control in that region, small churches have come into being and, by their devotion, the women incarnate the love of Christ. They are a beautiful example of 'nameless saints' buried in a society for its healing.

In the following account, a minister describes the way his church is seeking to live as seed, yeast and salt in their neighbourhood. The emphasis is on warm personal friendships and a social life which is truly local in scale and flavour. He writes:

> This is the stuff of the local church ... all fairly mundane yet it affirms what people already are in God's providence rather than presenting them with an illusive media-generated ideal. In an age when only the large-scale and dramatic is seen as important, this is an approach where the churches reflect the gospel of Jesus, 'an incarnate nobody'! These, to my mind, are the real 'signs and wonders'!

He goes on to give an intriguing instance of 'local namelessness' over against the warping effects of 'Big Name Fame'.

> The contrast is evident to me in the recent fashion show that Pam organised. The models were all like the women who attended ... ordinary women of a variety of shapes and sizes, wearing clothes most other women present could see themselves clothed in. This contrasts sharply with the TV catwalks populated by androgynous skeletons attired in obscure outfits that few can either identify with or ever see themselves wearing. To press

the analogy, I think that much of our Christian spirituality of the past thirty years or so has actually been somewhat enthralled to this idealising of the unusual. Yet here we have found that growth has come through the reverse, and I suspect this is because it is this sort of spirituality that actually empowers people.

The hiddenness of spiritual germination, fermentation and seasoning begins when we commit ourselves to people, a street, a district or a place of work. Such commitment requires a sense of call and purpose, a recognition that the Lord has placed us there. Love, care, identification with others and prayer all play a part.

At Conisbrough, the congregation were committed to being:

...a church that prayed, cared and shared. This would mean that the whole parish would eventually be covered by individuals praying, caring and sharing. Every person within the community, young and old, rich or poor, in work or out of work, could be included in prayer, and everyone in the church would pray ... Each person was to see himself or herself as a light on their street, to friends, neighbours and relatives ... We were encouraged to identify people to pray for, then to commit ourselves to pray for them daily. One lady not only offered to pray for her own street, but also adopted a nearby one. From the adopted street of about forty homes, ten people started coming to church during the first year. Five of these have since been confirmed.[2]

A fine example of Christ's nameless saints living as the means of his healing in their community.

To live in this hidden way requires that we be content (not complacent) with who we are and where we are; that we recognise God's purposes for us in our present situation; that we are not always fretting to be someone else, somewhere else. The source of our contentment is the knowledge that our lives have real value and significance through God's engagement with the people around us. We are content to be unknown because we are profoundly known to the Lord who is working through us.

Professor William Abraham describes an encounter that a Christian friend of his had with another passenger on a flight. By the time they reached their destination, his fellow traveller expressed his desire to follow Christ. As they were parting at the airport, the man said to the Christian who had led him to faith, 'By the way, don't be too proud about what you have done for me. You must be the twentieth person this year who has spoken to me about Christ!'

Few of us have the privilege of being the twentieth, but there would not have been a twentieth had there not been a first, a thirteenth, a seventeenth. Because nineteen people were content to be who they were, where they were, the chain of witness progressed to that golden moment experienced by number twenty on that plane.

Our ordinary, often anonymous lives take on tremendous significance when serving God's purposes. Significance and value are not had by snatching at them, but by following our Lord into powerful obscurity, working quietly in the world as its seed, yeast and salt.

Chapter 5

MISPHAT

Picture Israel at rock-bottom, defeated and servile as a consequence of her incorrigible fascination with Canaanite animism (Judges 6). We first meet Gideon scrabbling around inside a winepress, trying to conceal his family's wheat from the voracious Bedouin Midianites who dominated the region. Gideon's circumstances made him a disappointed believer. He treated the angel's greeting like a joke made in poor taste (v 12): he certainly did not feel like a 'mighty warrior'. His response was charged with bitterness and anger as he compared what God ought to be doing for his people with their actual dire circumstances (v 13). Here is the cynicism of the defeated, disillusioned believer.

Too much disappointment sucks the vitality out of faith. In fact, 'disappointment' is a polite way of implying that our faith has failed us. Is this one weakness too far? The weakness of being trapped in discouraging circumstances, while the chemistry of disappointment leaves us hurt and cynical?

Gideon is an unlikely candidate for national saviour: 'My clan is the weakest in Manasseh, and I am the least in my family' (v 15). Yet God persists. The divine call is fantastic in its audacity: 'Go in the strength you have and save Israel'. Before Gideon could protest that he had not a scrap of strength for any such task, God completed the command with the assurance which measures the future: 'Am I not sending you?'

Thus far we are on familiar territory: a poor and powerless person is taken up and set to work within God's purposes. Gideon was released from his cynicism to lead the struggle for the nation's soul (vs 25–40). But it is the next phase of his preparation which interests us, particularly because in it we discover the secret of the effectiveness that lies within weakness.

Gideon was instructed to reduce his army of national liberation from 32,000 to 10,000 and then down to a mere 300 (7:1–8). Yet he was still able to triumph in a brilliant night attack.

The usual lesson drawn from this episode is that, with God, quality counts above quantity. In the Christian life we should stop counting and start weighing. And this is sound advice, from a perfectly valid reading of the story. But it is not its primary lesson, nor is it simply that God is powerful enough to do whatever he intends. (In which case, the story would make God out to be like the strong man at the fair, who tears up telephone directories with his bare hands – awesome to behold but rather pointless.)

Gideon – down to his last 300 fighters against 'the Midianites, the Amalekites and all the other eastern peoples ... thick as locusts', 'their camels could no more be counted than the sand on the seashore' (7:12) – is a sign to us of misphat. Misphat is one of a rich cluster of terms at the core of God's covenant relationship with his people. It is the Hebrew term for 'what is right, the right way for God to act, God's rightness'. God acts upon the world according to his misphat, which is why, in scripture, his people celebrate him as the God of the poor and the weak.

God may be able to resist the appeals of the rich, the powerful, the satiated, but he will never, can never, resist the prayers of his 'poor ones'. Gideon, disarmed and hopelessly vulnerable before powerful Midian; Gideon, 'the weakest' and 'the least' of a defeated, despairing people, is in the strongest possible position with God; because the Lord, in his rightness and justice (his misphat), is on the side of the weak and oppressed. That is his nature, and our well-being flows from that unchangeable fact about him.

'He has filled the hungry with good things'

Gideon proved the truth which is fundamental to our own life with God, that the weakness which can overwhelm us does not disqualify us from his fellowship and service. On the contrary, it qualifies us! The gentle, just and compassionate treatment of the poor and the weak – those who are stuck in their circumstances, incapable of enforcing their own rights – lies at the very heart of God's covenant requirements. It decides the way he treats us and the way we are to treat one another. Hence the familiar covenant formula of God's commitment to 'the poor and the oppressed, the widows and orphans' (most clearly articulated in Isaiah 1:16–17,23; 3:14; 5:20–23; 28:17; 32:1,16–20, where misphat makes the transition to shalom).

God is the source of misphat; rightness and justice are the fruit of his compassion (Isaiah 51:3,8). Raising up the poor involves laying low the rich and satiated. And it is the 'servant of the Lord' who becomes the special mediator of God's misphat to the whole world (42:1–4), which he can do only by suffering himself (53:11). Thus God acts out his misphat. He is bound to come to the poor, to stand with them and take up their cause.

Now we can see why God stripped Gideon down to his tiny force. The stress is not upon the might of the 300 men but upon God's covenant commitment to bewildered, oppressed Israel – his misphat, whereby he must join his people in their sicknesses and raise them up into the life and power of his purposes.

We may be tempted to wonder if the work of the kingdom would not progress faster if God gave a little less time to his weak and poor! One writer suggests, 'God's weariness at the sin of the world brings him into an ever deeper solidarity with the weary. Perhaps it is because he is treated so shamefully in his covenant that he loves from the very beginning to be with those who are weakened and treated shamefully.'

Mary's song is the classic expression of God's *misphat* love:

'He has brought down rulers from their thrones
    but has lifted up the humble.
He has filled the hungry with good things
    but has sent the rich away empty.'
(Luke 1:52–53)

Jesus – God's *misphat* incarnate

Jenny Barnes, a prison chaplain, describes for us a critical moment in her ministry, when the loving misphat of the Lord dawned upon her in relation to the people around her:

This is really a story of my own arrogance and spiritual pride. My first experience of preaching was to set the scene for the rest of my ministry. I had been invited to preach at the main Sunday service in a prison in North Yorkshire. I was all prepared to preach a very hard-hitting sermon about sinfulness, selfishness, guilt and the need to repent 'earnestly' of these things. I believed that these men were obviously guilty of great sinfulness and evil, and I was the one to tell them. As I sat in the chapel, a converted army hut, I looked out at the men who were sitting there, about seventy of them, and I saw for the first time an intensity of pain, anger, sadness, frustration that I really had never seen before. All of these emotions were there in the body language of the men, but most of all in their eyes. I sat there as the service progressed with a growing sense of discomfort. I gradually began to realise that these men already knew of their own sinfulness, selfishness, their own guilt, their own lack of self-worth. It was written all over their faces. In that short space of time God taught me a lesson that I have never forgotten. He showed me that my own pride and arrogance was just as bad, if not worse, than what I had assumed about the prisoners.

God spoke clearly to me that morning and I was changed in an instant. Since that day I have spent many hours with men in prison. I have shared with them some of their deepest pain and hurt, and have experienced something of their desperate needs. Of course they are not perfect, but neither am I! There has to be a mutual understanding that we all need God's love and forgiveness, and that we are all basically in the same boat.

I have come to understand that it is only from the position of my own weakness that I can minister in any environment, be it in prison or parish. Getting alongside, sharing good times and bad, meeting physical needs, sorting out family problems, just being there is what will really begin to open our eyes to the love God has for everything he created. The Christian gospel is not concerned just with giving out penalties for wrongdoing or exacting revenge for pain and loss inflicted on others, nor even to make offenders 'smart' in order to teach them a lesson. The Christian gospel is concerned with Jesus Christ who bore the burden of sin in order to transform character, and who absorbed evil in order to redeem someone precious in his sight.

Needless to say, I did not preach the sermon I had prepared for those prisoners that day in North Yorkshire. Instead I told them of God's unconditional love for each one of us, and especially for them!

God's misphat in Christ is the great leveller. We are all saved by it, and it sets the tone and character of our lives and ministry. From now on, boundless generosity towards God's poor will be the authentic sign of our witness.

Beyond disappointment

It is delightful to meet Christians and congregations who are flourishing and growing. It is, if anything, even more wonderful – certainly more mysterious and awe-inspiring – to meet those who seem to flourish against all odds in circumstances we might regard as oppressively disappointing. This surely is a sign of God's misphat, his closeness to his poor and weak ones.

When Oscar and Emilie Schindler (of Schindler's List fame) were fleeing from the Russians, they stayed one night in a bombed-out hotel. Emilie writes:[1]

I went into our room and saw on the table an old book in red leather binding, which turned out to be a Bible. What was a Bible doing there? I opened it at random to a passage in the book of Jeremiah:

'For who shall have pity upon thee, O Jerusalem? ... their widows were increased ... terrors upon the city...'

This is God's answer to the terrible words of the prophet:

'And I will deliver thee out of the hand of the wicked, and I will redeem thee out of the hand of the terrible.'

Suddenly my hopes were reborn. In the midst of so much desolation, I had received a message. As the sky was turning darker, a strange radiance was brightening my heart, until then laden with sombre thoughts by the feeling that all roads were being closed off to us, that there was no escape.

Emilie had touched the misphat love of God.

Chapter 6

THE CHILD, THE CLOWN AND
THE PIED PIPER

Power is a quality steeped in mystique. It is also feared and loathed because of the misery caused by its abuse, both inside the church as well as outside. Yet 'the kingdom of God is not a matter of talk but of power' (1 Cor 4:20).

Before we read our own ideas of power back into these words of the apostle Paul, we should attend to Jesus' astonishing definition. Of all the symbols and pictures he could have used to suggest the essential character of discipleship, he chose from his own memories of childhood. Life in the kingdom, he said, is clothed in the enchanted vulnerability of a child (Matt 18:1–4; 19:13–15). God the King is God the Father, and we seriously misrepresent the nature of his kingdom unless we see it as the loving rule of a father over his children.

To be 'weak enough for God to use' includes the startling idea that we should be childlike enough for him to bless – or, rather, childlike enough to receive his blessing. However, to be childlike – to be as a child before God – does not mean to be infantile. We do not have to act like those Christians in fifteenth-century Switzerland, who took Jesus' words literally and, as adults, played nursery games with dolls and toys.

In Luke's version of Jesus' teaching, one characteristic of childhood is stressed – the child's natural ability to receive gifts: 'anyone who will not receive the kingdom of God like a little child will never enter it' (Luke 18:15–17). We tend to grow out of the child's receptivity. As adults, we often feel awkward and embarrassed when given gifts, perhaps even a little suspicious, as if it implies some need on our part. Children show how it should be done. They receive presents without any inhibitions, with naturalness and laughter, as if the whole point of life is to receive good things from loving people. In this, they touch the heart of the kingdom.

> 'I praise you, Father, Lord of heaven and earth, because you have hidden these things from the wise and learned, and revealed them to little children.'
>
> *(Matthew 11:25)*

Luke strikes the contrast between childlike receptivity and adult frigidity in his account of the rich man who is quite unable to allow himself to receive eternal life as the Father's gift to his child (Luke 18:18–25). His question, 'What must I do to inherit' the gift, assumes that, like most things in life, it is all a matter of passing examinations. His hands are too full with possessions, prestige and self-sufficiency to receive the gift of God.

It is not difficult to apply this picture to our Christian lives. We are conditioned by adulthood to regard the receiving of gifts as child's play, while 'real men' graft for their blessings. Discipleship becomes a rather grim business of working on the kingdom assembly line. We enter the Christian life justified by faith, but then spend the rest of our days striving to justify ourselves by works.

The Christian life is nothing other than allowing oneself to receive what is bestowed by God's boundless love and generosity. 'Everything is gift – the receiver of the gift is himself the first gift received' (philosopher Gabriel

Marcel), a profound insight which children know by instinct.

Perhaps Jesus had in mind those strange culinary arrangements, with manna and quail, during Israel's desert march . They describe perfectly a childlike dependence upon the Father for each new day. God did not send Israel across the wilderness with freezers stocked with forty years' supply of food. Who needs to depend upon God when cupboards are full? Instead he broke up their journey into one day at a time and covenanted to meet them each day with 'enough for that day' (Exod 16:4). We are to take each day – each precious, precarious, dangerous, unrepeatable day – from God's hands as his personal gift from father to child. Those who accept each day like trustful children, as a gift, will see it coming from God brimming with newness and love and possibility. But the jaded adult mind will see only one more predictably boring day.

Playfulness, freedom and laughter

If we can shift from our usual self-reliance to the child's dependence on God (and only the Holy Spirit can work this change in us), other childlike characteristics will arise in our lives: a real playfulness, freedom from killing anxieties, and laughter (Matt 6:25–34) – three blessings which virtually constitute the Holy Grail for our unhappy society.

Just occasionally we encounter or hear about people who do seem able to live as children before the Father. In the Middle Ages, Francis of Assisi reacted to the dissolute opulence of the church by founding a joyous community of mendicants, who roamed the streets 'with the innocent abandon of lilies of the field'. And Hudson Taylor, in China, was intensely concerned with simplicity of faith, without which, he said, given the dangers and stresses of their lives, 'missionaries would sometimes die or become insane':[1]

> The Lord's will is that all His people should be an unburdened people, fully supplied, strong, healthy and happy ... It is the Lord's will that his people should be as a child of the king ... there are few things more attractive than joy, and few more communicative. We are instinctively drawn to persons possessed of a happy countenance and a bright cheery manner. Who does not know what it is to find depression and gloom disappearing before them? They do indeed 'scatter beams of sunshine' ... when all is in His hand all will be safe, all will be wisely dealt with, all will be done, and well done.

It takes a cheerful, childlike trust to undertake certain kinds of work wholeheartedly, without worrying too much about the outcome. It requires a vision of our whole life continually thrown into the air in praise, in the trust that it will be caught, blessed, and return renewed. There is often a touch of the clown about such people.

A Muslim taxi driver in Rotherham was startled to see a group of people with buckets surround his car. They insisted on washing his windscreen. When he tried to pay them something they refused, explaining that they were Christians from the local church who just wanted to do this small thing for him out of love. He told them he had been years in England and this was the first time a Christian had done anything for him.

A group of young people in a Sheffield church meet for prayer on a Saturday morning before going out with their brooms to sweep the streets of the parish out of love for God and the local people.

In the Philippines, Melba Maggay calls this same spirit of childlike clownishness, 'playing the Pied Piper'.[2] She and some other Christians were seized by the great idea of calling together as many churches and Christian groups as possible, to work for social change. There were objections – 'Who are we anyway to mobilise the evangelicals?' – and a feeling that such a movement would require huge organisation. But Melba responded, 'Never mind. Let us issue a call and let him who hears hear it. Play the Pied Piper, sing a tune that people will recognise as their own.' It was God's moment and the response was incredible: 'As a mother cuddling a child said to me, "We just want to be here."'

Truly creative movements do not need huge organisations to carry them forward. Listen, look, discern what the Lord is doing and the tune he is playing. 'We played the flute for you and you did not dance ... (Matt 11:17). The childlike imagination is most receptive to this vision of life.

'He brought all newness with him'

Small children grow into young people. A young Christ burst in upon a tired world made old by sin. Our Lord Jesus is that fabulous child seen with his Father laying down the playground of creation: 'Then I was at [God's] side each day, his darling and delight, playing in his presence continually, playing over his whole world while my delight was in mankind' (Prov 8:30–31, REB). Scratch the surface of creation and you come upon delight, joy, playfulness, which are its meaning bestowed upon it by Christ, the Logos. When Christ's human family vandalised the playground and spoilt the game, he came to show us an even lovelier way: 'Know that he brought all newness with him when he brought himself' (Irenaeus). The Gospels are charged with his new love, his new wine bursting through the old skins; his words and works, his imagination and vision could come only out of a young mind. He was always young, even at his death: 'And if the Spirit of him who raised Jesus from the dead is living in you, he who raised Christ from the dead will also give life to your mortal bodies through his Spirit, who lives in you' (Rom 8:11). The Holy Spirit of the young Christ makes his life real in us, pushing against the spirit of ageing and the spirit of the age.

To be a Christian is to be profoundly young. This truth has nothing to do with the rather sad picture of old people pretending to be young. Christ's young life in us by his Spirit means we are always standing at the threshold of God's new purposes, with eternity stretching out undiminished before us.

The child and the young teenager are often regarded as weak, volatile, vulnerable, ungrounded and insecure. But consider Christ's great precursor, David, when he saved Israel by his duel with Goliath (1 Sam 17). Where was King Saul at that moment, whose job it was to defend Israel? He took one look at Goliath and decided he was too big to fight. David took one look and decided he was too big to miss. Yet Saul was once a David in terms of potential, 'an impressive young man without equal among the Israelites' (9:2). What went wrong? Saul grew out of that passion for the glory of God, which David never lost – the boy's outrageous optimism as he shed conventional weapons and selected his five pebbles (17:37,46).

Saul became cautious, calculating, pragmatic. He grew out of his young vision into a disenchanted, sad adult. This process threatens each of us. We settle for becoming competent, 'professional' – perhaps we even attain some technical mastery of the Christian faith – but those are old words, safe words, unlikely to take on the Goliaths of this world and far removed from young David's holy intoxication with the glory of God, his passionate desire to please and be pleased by the Lord. He acted decisively while the adults stood around, confused and powerless, embarrassed by his audacious faith.

At that moment, David displayed the newness which is Christ's gift to us by his Holy Spirit: 'Know that he brought all newness with him when he brought himself'. Newness in creative vision, a playful inventiveness, open (like children) to strange and surprising combinations, sometimes a touch eccentric, a bit extreme, reckless enough to make 'sensible' people shake their heads.

> While many become Christians because of the security there is in Christ, and many within the church seek nothing more than a homely dullness, there are many others who long to take risks for Christ. Both young and old need the opportunity to be *peregrinati* – to venture new things for Christ. They may achieve much or nothing. They may be hurt or helped in the attempt, but whatever happens they will have grown in knowing the ways of God, discovering themselves as people and adding to their store of experience.
>
> *(John Finney)*[3]

In Belfast, Gary Mason despaired of the entrenched suspicion within his community, even between Christian groups. Gary and others decided to go beyond religious, political and social divisions. Together they have formed a 'reconciliation centre' in the Shankhill Road, literally on the boundary between Catholic and Protestant communities – in the firing line in more than one sense. When denounced by his Christian critics, who accuse him of compromising their principles, Gary replies:[4]

> Shouldn't the followers of Christ be known as peacemakers? ... Isn't it better to make friends than

enemies? ... To have a particular flag is to be filled with pride and insecurity .... Raising the banner of love is to tell an alternative way of seeing and doing ... we do not say we are 'Christians' but we are 'family'.

And a little child will lead them.
(Isaiah 11:6)

Chapter 7

'THE SOFT, BARELY AUDIBLE SOUND OF ALMOST BREATHING'

Look carefully at a violin and you will observe that it is mostly empty space. In gifted hands, its shaped emptiness is capable of incredible sound. The idea that emptiness can live and be useful, even beautiful, is astonishing and profound.

On the walls of the catacombs, the first Christians portrayed Christ as Orpheus, the fabulous musician who could charm the wild beasts out of the forests with his irresistible music. Jesus can take up the dull instrument of our emptiness and make it play for him.

We read in the Bible how the Lord works his magic on different personalities – people like Elijah, at the end of his tether, waiting for God to touch him afresh and make his exhausted emptiness sing. Elijah had spent himself vindicating God against the prophets of Baal (1 Kings 18). From that ecstatic high, he descended swiftly into the crashing low of post-battle exhaustion. He fled for his life from Jezebel and collapsed, drained, depressed and near suicidal: 'I have had enough, Lord ... Take my life' (1 Kings 19:1–5). Revived by an angel, his prophet's homing instinct led him to the traditional holy place of theophanies, to Horeb, God's mountain, where the Lord had revealed himself in fire to Moses. There he waited for God, for a fresh encounter which would empower and direct him towards God's purposes.

The Lord would come, Elijah assumed, in classic signs and wonders, in pyrotechnics and spectacular convulsions in nature, awesome symbols of the divine power and glory. In other words, he looked for God through the usual channels. And God did indeed give him his expected display of natural violence, with winds, earthquake and fire, greater than any yet. But God was in none of it!

A strange thing was happening to Elijah: his idea of the way God reveals himself is actually disconfirmed in this great display of power. God is not, after all, in the tempest, the earthquake and the fire of Elijah's traditional world-view.

This is a critical moment for Elijah. If he insists on his old, static perception, in which God always comes along the same traditional lines – in explosions of high electricity and mega-decibels measuring six on the Richter scale – then the development of Elijah's faith will stop dead. It is a mark of his spiritual greatness that he is not destroyed by those impressive but empty phenomena; rather, he waits for God to come however he might come.

Open to a new voice

Elijah's weakness became a door to a possibility unlike anything he had expected, that God can come also in 'a gentle whisper' (v 12); except that 'gentle whisper' is a rather limp translation of the original text, which attempts to explain the inexplicable, to make clear something which is obscure, ambiguous and strange. Literally, the Hebrew says that Elijah heard 'a voice of thin silence', or 'a small voice of silence'. The Authorised Version keeps faith with the haunting suggestiveness of the original with its famous 'still small voice'. Rabbi Lawrence Kushner renders it, 'the soft, barely audible sound of almost breathing', something like the sound of Elijah's own breathing, as close and personal as that.[1] Yet it was also a voice communicating a message, for the outcome was no less significant than if the Lord had revealed himself in violent phenomena. Elijah was set upright again and directed back north to organise a double coup d'état in Syria and Israel (1 Kings 20). By the 'still, small voice', God continued to shape history.

As I look at the account of Elijah's experience, I am aware that something similar happened in my own life when I was working in East Asia as a missionary. In common with many other missionaries, I perceived God as, supremely, the Great Evangelist, concerned chiefly with mission and missions, conversions and church planting.

Then came my 'Horeb' moment. My family became so ill that we had no choice but to return home – from a ministry we loved and in which we seemed to be needed and useful. If it is not too pompous to dare to say, I could well identify with Elijah's despair: 'I have been very zealous for the Lord ... and now they are trying to kill me too' (1 Kings 19:10). I was at my wit's end – unwell, confused and quite unable to find the Lord as I searched for him desperately through my usual channels of communication.

My view of God at that stage was too small, too much shaped by a certain kind of missionary hagiography and some of the fantasies often associated with missionary service. My view of God was not big enough to cover the chaotic mess we found ourselves in. We went through a nightmare which shook and exposed my excessively activist faith. If God was the supreme mission strategist, if he had called me to that area of service within his mission, why were we breaking down under the stress of what was, after all, his work done at his call?

My view of God was, in fact, my version of the Tempest-God and Fire-God of Elijah's traditional worldview. Yet God was not to be found in those categories.

Gradually, over a period of a couple of years, quietly, the 'soft, barely audible sound of almost breathing' arose in my mind. It was the picture in scripture of the Lord sitting at his potter's wheel, working with the difficult clay of his people (Isaiah 45:9; Jer 18:1-6). I believe I had always known this image, but now it became a vital presence in the centre of my thoughts, slowly bringing the chaos to order through healing and illumination.

Whatever tricks the clay may throw up, the potter is able to master and compel them to serve his design. Sickness? Failure? Uselessness? Emptiness? Rebellion and sin? They are flaws in the clay, which draw out from his fingers yet more and more answering skill. Never for a second does he cease to interact with the clay on the wheel as it takes shape. If one should stop him halfway through and comment that his work on the wheel does not look like much, he will answer, 'I haven't finished yet. Be patient! Wait! You will see!'

The potter, I realised as I thought about this parable, actually blends himself with the clay, pours himself into it through his fingers. He masters the blips and faults, the sudden changes of texture and colour, in such a way that when the pot is eventually fired, those 'flaws' which threatened the project are now seen to be integral to the design. Indeed, it is as if the design required those disorders!

The 'still, small voice' for me was the dawning realisation that God is not a production manager with his blueprints and schedules, his graphs and ten-year plans. He is the artist who takes into his hands the whole messy reality of our lives, with all our weaknesses, inabilities and eccentricities. He is able to persuade it all towards the picture he has of us in his imagination. The whispered word arising in my meditation on scripture brought the understanding that, in Julian's lovely words, 'all shall be well and all manner of thing shall be well'.

The 'voice of thin silence' of the Holy Spirit did not come out of my customary lines of thought, but from an unexpected direction. It heralded a new departure for me in my relationship with God. It suggested a spirituality different from my activist-dominated view of the Christian life. In fact, what was happening was not the rejection of my 'missionary' world-view but its correction and enlargement. God's mission to the world is (as Isaiah and Jeremiah especially reveal) to form his mind in the mind of the nations. Far from being in opposition to his seeking and saving love in the world, the Lord as potter is the ultimate missionary parable. It views God not as merely 'saving souls', but as forming the image of Jesus his Son in the peoples of the world. The divine potter is the great Evangelist, and the good news is that the world and its history are ceaselessly being shaped by the nail-pierced hands of him who is 'making everything new' (Rev 21:5).

I believe that the Lord's 'still, small voice' became a practical reality in my life only because my weakness and emptiness opened the door to it. As I read the letters people have sent me, with descriptions of their diverse stories, it occurs to me that the 'small voice of silence', or 'the voice of thin silence', is so called because it speaks to those experiences which are too deep and elusive to tell. Yet they are the most real part of us. The voice is discerned when a person's usual channels of communication with God seem to have fallen silent. As Elijah discovered, the crisis of faith became, in the love of God, a door to new faith, an unexpected communion with the Lord, a new commissioning to service.

I give one more example – a heartbreaking experience, yet within it are clues that, against all reason, the still, small voice has been heard. This is from a young grandmother:

As far as our little granddaughter is concerned, the struggle goes on. At seven months, she still weighs only 8 lbs, cannot hold her head up, has very little sight and has just come out of another few days in hospital. She is home on a monitor.

I am beginning to see things more clearly in retrospect. At first there was the anxiety and shock, and sadness, that this was the price tag for intervention techniques that 'hang on' to babies who threaten to arrive too prematurely – most of which go on to develop normally, but for the few there was a reason for the early labour.

After the initial response there followed for me strange inexplicable feelings and general malaise. Eventually, as I sat and wept in the garden, I was able to explain to my husband that I knew where the highland folklore about 'changelings' had come from. The notion that the fairies had exchanged one of their sickly infants for a healthy human one described exactly how I felt – cheated, as though something good had been snatched away and exchanged for a mass of difficulties that were not intended. I simultaneously wanted to save my daughter and her husband from all the exhaustion and heartache of a badly disabled child by rubbing out what was wrong, yet I felt extraordinarily protective of my granddaughter.

God has made nothing better in physical terms, only in the gradual blurring of the lines between right and wrong, good and bad, intended and spoilt, and in enabling us to accept all the jarring elements as part of a blessed whole. In one way it's hard to wait five months for a granddaughter's first smile, especially when her mother seemed to smile at five days, but there is enormous joy in that too.

The voice which whispers in the heart 'enabling us to accept all the jarring elements as part of a blessed whole', spoke also to a man who struggled much of his life against depression, at times to the edge of madness. The poet-priest, Gerard Manley Hopkins, discovered that God does speak with 'a crash' but also with 'a lingering-out sweet skill'; that he is not a one-track, monochrome deity, but comes to us in...

All things counter, original, spare, strange;
Whatever is fickle, freckled (who knows how?)
With swift, slow; sweet, sour; adazzle, dim.[2]

It is a happy cliché (and true) that the Lord speaks to us in the things that are 'swift, sweet, adazzle'. However, we need to listen for 'the soft, barely audible sound of almost breathing' to discern him also in the 'slow, sour, dim' things which make up so much of our experience.

Chapter 8

LOVE WITH A SHAKEN MIND

In one of his Hasidic stories,[1] Elie Wiesel tells how the great Rebbe, Israel Baal Shem Tov (Master of the Good Name), stormed into God's presence one day and demanded action: God must send his Messiah to earth now, without further delay. Satan was furious and complained that the Rebbe's behaviour was outrageous. God was inclined to agree that Baal Shem Tov had indeed overstepped the mark and ought to be taught a lesson. The Rebbe and his faithful scribe were packed off to a remote island where they at once fell into the hands of pirates.

'Do something, Master!' cried the scribe. 'Exert your power! Say a word! Get us out of here!'

But the Rebbe was powerless. His secret knowledge and extraordinary spiritual gifts had vanished. He could remember nothing and do nothing. He was empty.

'Never mind,' said the Rebbe. 'You surely can remember some of my wisdom and my words of power. Recite a prayer or an incantation.'

But the scribe found that he was as empty as his master. He could think of nothing – nothing except 'A, B, C...' Yes, he could with effort just about recall the beginning of the alphabet.

'Then do it,' said the Master of the Good Name. 'Say it, and I will repeat it after you.'

Together they slowly recited the aleph, beith, gimmel,

daleth of the Hebrew alphabet, 'the sacred letters which together contain all the mysteries of the universe'. As they recited the letters over and over, their strength returned. The joy of the Lord flooded their hearts, and they found themselves off that miserable island and safely back home, a lot wiser.

Love is the ABC

'Isolated amnesiacs' is a stark but not unfair description of us much of the time. We live forgetful that love is our meaning. The best defence Jesus could offer of himself and his gospel was the fact of his loving people. His work is only credible when his followers strive to make the love of Christ the basis for everything they do:

> 'A new command I give you: Love one another. As I have loved you, so you must love one another. By this all men will know that you are my disciples, if you love one another.'
> *(John 13:34–35)*

Love is the radiant centre of life in Christ, from which, in our folly, we drift away. The consequences are isolation, fear, feebleness and a lost sense of the Lord's loving presence. Healing comes as we recover the fundamentals of love – the ABC of our life with God.

Is love strength or weakness? Anything which 'always protects, always trusts, always hopes, always perseveres' (1 Cor 13:7) must possess extraordinary energies. But it is an upside-down sort of power when set alongside prevailing views of personal dynamism. Love has the strength to kneel and serve, and, in that sense, to dare to appear weak in relation to other people. Christ's love means bearing the burden of love: 'God so loved the world that he gave his one and only Son' (John 3:16); 'since God so loved us, we also ought to love one another' (1 John 4:11). We must make our way back to the radiant simplicity of love's ABC.

In a pile of routine newsletters, I noticed this one from Thailand:[2]

A few years later, a girl of seventeen, with badly clawed hands, came to the clinic along the unsurfaced red clay paths. She had the worst type of leprosy, with four limbs affected. Leprosy was also affecting her eyes and, without treatment, she would become blind. This meant visiting her in her own home to give frequent check-ups. One day she told me of a young man living nearby, PSP, who was severely affected by leprosy. We started anti-leprosy treatment. He was in his late twenties and had recognisable leprosy from when he was circumcised at thirteen, so probably he had contracted it some twenty years before we encountered him.

One day I woke with a compelling force – I must go to see PSP, even though he had his medical supplies. A colleague and I made our journey along the main road, side road, dusty path to his hut. He was dying. The family, seeing his hopeless condition and appalling leprosy, had decided to leave it to the will of Allah and let him die. His disease was going through a phase of exacerbation. He had huge ulcers, the size of plates. I let out basins of pus, which my colleague disposed of in the bushes as there was no sanitation or drain system at all. We bought him nutritious drinks and made arrangements to take him into our small in-patient unit as soon as possible. There he responded to the gospel of love and became a firm believer.

A similar situation arose some time later. At the rural hospital, I was holding a fortnightly clinic. A plump young lady, B, with many medical problems, was coming for regular treatment. One day she failed to turn up. As I ate my lunch, I felt I must go and visit this girl in her home, some 18 km away. It was as though I could hear the Lord saying, 'You must go to see B.' But I was to take the afternoon clinic. What could I do?

I asked a doctor to stand in for me. I drove along the country paths in second and third gear, and eventually reached her village. I found her literally burning with fever. The mercury in the thermometer could barely register the raging fever. As I touched her I felt my hands burning. She obviously needed intravenous fluids and hospital treatment immediately, so we took her into our small unit. She too has learned to love the Lord and to serve him.

So much love, so much time, skill and energy given to help a few people at the bottom of the social pile. As Gary Mason said about life on the Shankhill Road in Belfast, 'Love is to tell an alternative way of seeing and doing', an alternative way with power. And yet we read of churches redirecting their financial support away from areas in the developing world, 'where nothing is happening', to other apparently more responsive projects. This is an indication of just how muddled we are about the practice of servant-minded love. Because we are confused, we lapse quite naturally into the pattern of power with which we are most familiar. Who in the financial world wouldn't move his money around for the best returns? American rock star, Michael Been, once looked into big business and into big churches, and concluded, 'Everything that goes on in every major corporation goes on inside the Church, except as a sideline the Church teaches religion.'

But then we come up against the paradoxical image of a world-redeeming God who strides towards the transfiguration of all things at the coming again of Jesus Christ, yet who 'will not shout or cry out, or raise his voice in the streets. A bruised reed he will not break, and a smouldering wick he will not snuff out' (Isaiah 42:2–3). Extraordinarily gentle behaviour for a cosmic entrepreneur.

In this matter of love and power, to see ourselves as others see us is an illuminating, if painful, exercise. The Japanese missionary theologian, Kosuke Koyama, wonders why the missionary enterprise from the Western churches to the East over the past four hundred years has made such little headway. He believes it is due to the wrong sort of crusading done in a spirit of superiority, which conceals within it contempt for the culture and sensitivities of those on the receiving end of mission. He graciously speaks as one of us:[3]

> We need to repent ... We are far more arrogant than people on the streets. We are bigoted. We are prestige minded ... We want to teach but we do not want to learn ... The Christian faith does not and cannot be spread by crusading. It will be spread without money, without bishops, without theologians, without planning, if people see a crucified mind, not a crusading mind, in Christians.

In other words, we must return to the fundamentals of Christ's love.

We cannot avoid the uncomfortable fact that intensely believing people may be oddly myopic about their denial of love and the consequent abuse of power and privilege. The old ruling class of South Africa, for example, who conceived and applied apartheid, were mostly Dutch Reformed Christians. At the other end of the spectrum, where post-modern Christian groups pursue their avant-garde experiments in liturgy, fellowship and outreach, a failure of love is equally possible. A colleague of mine helped with counselling people affected by the sad collapse of the Nine O'Clock Service in Sheffield. She told me of her distress and inner rage at revelations of how women had been manipulated in that organisation.

The crucified mind – a shaken mind

Love in action thinks with a crucified mind. It is not a clever mind, a philosophical mind, a religious mind, a mind steeped in knowledge or in wisdom. It is, says Kosuke Koyama, a 'shaken mind' which has encountered the love and holiness of God in Christ on the cross, and been fundamentally changed by it. The crucified mind has been shaken by the foolishness and weakness of God (1 Cor 1:23–25). The cross is now the measure of all things, and leads the believer towards a distinctive stance: 'genuine, yet regarded as impostors; known, yet regarded as unknown; dying, and yet we live on; beaten, and yet not killed; sorrowful, yet always rejoicing; poor, yet making many rich; having nothing, and yet possessing everything' (2 Cor 6:8–10).

The crucified mind of love is a mind in tension, attuned to a counter-culture which denies the world out of love for the world. It is the mind of a servant but not a doormat. It has an instinct for service and for situations where Christ's love can be practised, which may involve painful and costly decisions.

A couple in Cambridge, after many years, decided to move from their church to another.

> The contrast between a large, high-profile, very 'Cambridge' church, and a new, small, rather down-at-heel, ugly modern one could not have been greater ... simply to go to a little-known church within the city may not have seemed very exciting or worthwhile (compared to missionaries going overseas). Nevertheless, we soon realised that, at our new church, we could do new things, serve in new and probably more important ways, that we could learn new things.

Love, they felt, demanded a depth of attention to people and their situations, which was one of the reasons they decided to join a more 'ordinary' congregation.

It seems that many people are finding that received Christian teaching in our churches is often difficult to square with the realities of day-to-day life they experience. The black-and-white polarities of youth somehow seem less firm as time goes on.

Love in particular

The love of Christ, which we are called to share in, is always personal and localised. The late Mother Teresa of Calcutta is a symbol of this kind of love. She was sometimes criticised by the professionals for not having a wider, more integrated strategy of rescue and care. But she was committed to individuals and the particularities of each one's life, and not to a general mass of humankind. The challenge is to break through the generalities, where people are pigeon-holed in the usual categories, in order to know fewer individuals very well.

> The desert is not remote in southern tropics,
> The desert is not only around the corner,
> The desert is squeezed in the tube-train next to you,
> The desert is in the heart of your brother.
>
> *(T S Eliot)*[4]

Love has the ability to look and see. What you look hard at seems to look hard at you. What you study closely radiates back a meaning which is unique because each manifestation of the world is somehow different from any other. Jesus honoured individuals by his penetrating attention. He looked hard at them. So, to Simon Peter, he could say what he was and what he would become (Matt 16:18–19). In the crush, he could ask, 'Who touched me?' Though the crowd might hem him in, he can still sense the desperate individual (Luke 8:42–48). The Lord calls us by name, not by category.

Conan Doyle's fictional detective, Sherlock Holmes, was tremendously popular with the working classes. He was in fact a five-star, copper-bottomed snob, a real elitist – yet the population could not get enough of him. Why? Because he saw people as distinct individuals at a time when the deadly uniformity of the Industrial Revolution was sweeping away individuality and eccentricity. Holmes saw that each person had a unique drama encoded in their appearance – a cap, shoes, blisters on hands, an intonation in the voice. He searched for the story in each person.

G K Chesterton said of Robert Browning that he did not love humanity, but he loved individual people:[5]

> His sense of the difference between one man and another would have made the thought of melting them into a lump called humanity simply loathsome and prosaic. It would have been to him like playing four hundred beautiful airs at once. The mixture would not combine all, it would lose all. Browning believed that to every man that ever lived upon this earth had been given a definite and peculiar confidence of God. Each one of us was engaged on secret service; each one of us had a peculiar message ... Our thoughts, our faces, our bodies, our hats, our boots, our tastes, our virtues, and even our vices, were more or less fragmentary and inadequate expressions.

This slow-paced, detailed and painstaking love looks at the world with the crucified mind of Christ, and honours the story in every individual. It is a love that echoes the love with which Christ has already loved the world. We join in doing what he has already done, and fulfil what he has already fulfilled.

Chapter 9

BY WAY OF EXCHANGED LIFE

The early church called the cross 'a sign of expansion', reaching out into the four winds of the universe. It is also the sign of exchanged life – Christ's life for ours, our life at his expense. The principle of exchanged life is that 'when love bestows itself, something other is allowed to be'.[1] It is at the centre of God's government of the world and of our relationships with one another.

We are saved by the life exchanged on the cross, and we are, at the same moment, marked by it. From now on our attitude and behaviour must be cruciform (Rom 6). The cross is our power and wisdom, the way to new and fruitful living. In the eyes of the world, the cross may seem like weakness and foolishness (1 Cor 1:20–25); but the world will never really understand why Christians live as they do, when those Christians are true to the exchanged life of the cross.

Far from being an arbitrary choice on God's part – as if he tossed a coin one day to decide how his creation would move towards its destiny – the principle of exchanged life chose itself as the only one possible. Our human nature, which bears the impress of God's image (however much defaced by sin), connects with the inner life of the Trinity, where inexhaustible love endlessly flows between Father, Son and Holy Spirit.

The dance of love overflows

When the Greek fathers meditated on the Trinity, and the love between Father, Son and Holy Spirit, they saw it as a dance. They coined the term perichoresis, or circular dance (choreo is the Greek word for 'dance', from which we get 'choreography'), to express the mutual giving and receiving of love between the divine persons. In this profound doctrine, they saw the Father, the Son and the Holy Spirit not in static terms, as some of our own analogies might suggest, but in an ecstatic, reciprocal bestowing; an exchange, as in a dance in which every movement of one partner is balanced by the harmonious response of the other. The Celtic church symbolised the movement of mutual love within the Godhead by the endless convolutions of the Celtic knot which adorns much modern jewellery.

In the dynamic symbol of the perichoresis, divine power is displayed not as sheer, naked, irresistible force, but rather as the power to give oneself totally – the power of inexhaustible, self-surrendering love which exists for the good and the delight of the other persons. Ecstatic love ('ecstatic' means 'to go out of oneself') pours out for the other, in which all is giving and there is no thought of taking: what one has is the gift of the other.

From the life of mutual love within the Holy Trinity come truths of immense significance for the way in which the world understands itself. God is ecstatic love. The Trinity's dance of love will not be contained, but flows out into cosmic creation. The world was born out of this outpouring. Father, Son and Holy Spirit did not need creation but, in love, opened up the dance and made space, infinite space, for the created order to enter ('In my Father's house are many rooms', John 14:2).

The atheist may regard the world as a bad joke, the accidental outcome of chance. The Christian who is rooted in and enlightened by Trinitarian faith knows otherwise, and sees creation moving as in a dance, a glorious thing all bloom and festal, a holy feast. What then do we expect to find at the heart of redeemed existence? Ecstatic delight, all orchestrated by the love which is expressed in the exchanged life.

Because we reflect in some measure the inner life of the Godhead, we know that God intends us to live the exchanged life in relation to other people. The love that energises the perichoresis, the exchanged life that allows others to live, is Christ's cruciform love: 'This is how we know what love is: Jesus Christ laid down his life for us. And we ought to lay down our lives for our brothers' (1 John 3:16).

The power of the kingdom, which we love to celebrate in our worship and in our marches, is the power of self-giving, self-surrendering love. It is the power to appear weak in the eyes of a thrusting culture. So when we call upon the Holy Spirit for empowerment, it must be for self-effacing, humble, cheerful service, by which others 'are allowed to be'.

When love bestows itself

God comes to people through people, through those who, out of love and at personal cost, make their lives available to others. There is no way round this principle, no way to avoid the inconvenience of giving up ourselves and our time to others. Ordinary daily tasks can only proceed by countless small acts of self-sacrifice. The simplest meal is possible only because someone has bothered to make it – to peel the potato, to boil the egg, to slice the cucumber, to bake the fish; not to mention the time and skill given by someone else to grow the vegetables, catch the fish, cook the meal. Everything you know was given to you by others – teachers, writers, those who set the example or who provided the inspiration. It is the principle of the exchanged life – my life for yours, your life for mine. Parents allow their children to take over their lives from the moment of conception. My parents gave their life for me; I give my life for my children. The principle holds true for all relationships, down to the most transitory encounters. When you stand back and hold open a door, allowing strangers to go ahead of you, your twenty-five seconds 'wasted' is their twenty-five seconds bonus.

The principle of the laid-down life, the exchanged life, is at the root of authentic living. Where it is understood and honoured between people, a civilised and harmonious life is possible. Where it is scorned (look around you), life becomes a harsh, isolated affair.

God comes to people through the self-giving love of people. Not one of us came to faith in Jesus Christ except through the influence of another person. So we cannot ask God to bless others and then stand coolly aloof, hiding behind church services or books, keeping them at arm's length. Not if we hope to be used by God.

In John Le Carré's novel, The Honourable Schoolboy, the spy Jerry Westerby is in a US airbase in Vietnam. He is surprised by the way the officers run the show:[2]

The windows overlooking the airfield were smoked and double glazed. On the runway, aircraft landed and took off without making a sound. This is how they tried to win, Jerry thought: from inside soundproof rooms, through smoked glass, using machines at arm's length. This is how they lost!

Christians are called to a more immediate engagement. The apostle Paul declared to the young church in Thessalonica, 'We loved you so much that we were delighted to share with you not only the gospel of God but our lives as well' (1 Thess 2:8). To share our lives with people is only possible if we come close enough to them and stand on the same level with them, without any hint of patronising superiority. In other words, if we stand in solidarity with them.

Love for – solidarity with

Back in chapter 5, Jenny Barnes described the moment in her ministry as prison chaplain when she realised that what she took to be her evangelistic love for the prisoners was in fact an attitude of power and superiority over them. When she acknowledged that, before anything else, we are all fellow sinners before our offended Father, her relationship with them was transformed into one of solidarity.

In Jesus, we see how authentic love for people requires that we share our lives with them. He is willing to be 'of the same family' as us; he is not ashamed to call us his brothers (Heb 2:11) and to stand in full solidarity with us as our sympathetic high priest (v 17). When he submitted to John's baptism of repentance (he who had nothing of which to repent), he stepped into the Jordan in order to identify fully with sinful, repenting human beings. His act of repentance was representative and vicarious: he repented on our behalf just as he did all things for our sakes, and finally died 'numbered with the transgressors' (Isaiah 53:12). And he calls us to follow his example: 'As the Father has sent me, I am sending you' (John 20:21).

Solidarity adds steeliness to love, makes love stubborn and persistent. Solidarity is love which will not let go or go away. Dom Helder Camara, a much-loved bishop in Brazil, urged Christians to the love which is free of all superior status and thereby invites people to walk with Christ:[3]

If we don't press the absurd claim of being the best, if we present ourselves as brothers and sisters for others, we shall be astounded to discover what a lot of people of good will there are about. Some of them may perhaps be rather timid, others will be so situated that they can't see things in the same light as we do. But once they come across somebody who speaks from the heart, not seeking to impose anything on them or humiliate them, and not with the conviction of being any cleverer or holier, then they are affected and would join the march.

The challenge to live in solidarity with others requires that we shed all pretence of self-sufficiency and are prepared to learn from so-called 'outsiders'. This may be a new and startling idea for many of us: Christians have often acted as though they had all the answers. But solidarity owns up to weakness without any fear of letting the gospel down.

Raymond Fung, who has looked closely at the 'love in solidarity' practised by churches around the world, writes of the mysterious power of vulnerability:[4]

A church communicating strength and power can be a provider of many useful services, but only a church that is not afraid of communicating weakness and need can draw people to God and build them up as full participants in the community of faith. That indeed is at the root of the methodology and spirituality of partnership...

While I was working in urban mission in the city of Hong Kong, I came to know a group of textile workers, mostly young women in their early twenties. They worked in the same plant and occasionally would gather for an evening of fun. About Christmas time, although only two out of the thirty were Christians, the group decided to do something 'Christian'. They settled on doing a Bible study on the Lukan version of the first Christmas. The Christians were very excited. They got in touch with us and made a detailed study with background material and questions for discussion and so on. But nothing like that happened. Once the young women got into Luke 2, most of them reading the Bible for the first time, they refused to follow our well-thought-out scheme. They were captured by one idea in the Christmas narrative – that Mary, the mother of Jesus, in pregnancy, had to travel a long distance, risking her health and the life of her baby. This was the point on which the young women's attention focused. They would not be drawn away.

Immediately they identified themselves with Mary. Like the mother of Jesus, they too had the experience of having their health and their yet-to-be-born babies put at risk because of the need to stay on the job until the last possible day. They were fascinated that Mary had to go through the same hardship. I could see their eyes brighten up. Their very mundane experience, to which nobody in Hong Kong gave a second thought, is in fact the experience of the mother of Jesus. How can it be? Are we after all so important?

At the time, labour legislation in Hong Kong provided for maternity leave, but without pay. So the law was totally meaningless. No working-class woman could afford to claim the leave. As a matter of fact, many women in the late months of their pregnancy would work overtime in order to save enough to tide over the post-delivery period when they could not work. The young women shared their experience and those of their friends. For the first time, they saw themselves in the world of Mary and Jesus. They realised that what they cared about, the Bible also cares about. Luke 2 did not provide a solution to the problem of pregnant workers. What

Luke 2 did was to embrace these workers and affirm their concerns.

The solution was obvious – to fight for an amendment to the existing law, to make the provision of maternity leave a paid provision. Thus began an organised effort by women workers to change the law. In ten months, the law was changed to provide two-thirds of the regular wage.

It was Mary's fragile situation and the real dangers facing the Holy Family – it was God's vulnerability – which so touched those young Hong Kong women. And it will be our vulnerability – our willingness to show that we too have needs, that we are not all strength and steel – which will reveal the power of the dance of love.

Chapter 10

BEFORE WORK

Modesty, says the proverb in a Christmas cracker, is the triumph of mind over flatter. Paul agrees: 'I say to every one of you: Do not think of yourself more highly than you ought' (Rom 12:3) – but how high or low that might be, he does not say. What is the measure of our worth?

A couple working in Indonesia hesitated to give an account of their story because, they said, they didn't think they had made much spiritual impact on the lives of the people around them. Were they being over-modest, or just realistic? Perhaps our effectiveness is the mark of our value as Christians, and we might interpret Paul's words as 'Do not think of yourself more highly than the evidence of the spiritual impact you have on others'.

Yet this view does not stand up to the passing of time. It fails to account for the way in which the Lord may allow our small boat to lie becalmed for considerable periods of time, during which we have little discernible spiritual impact on situations or people. To change metaphors, our car turns off the busy motorway into deserted side-streets and down a cul-de-sac.

Wise spiritual teachers tell us to embrace these fluctuations of our circumstances with faith and joy:

Nothing plays a greater role in God's pedagogical art than the shift from one extreme to the other ... this is

meant to ensure that we do not settle into any situation
but remain pliable, and to make us recognise that true
insight does not come from what we have grasped but
from ever greater readiness and deeper obedience.

(Hans Urs von Balthasar)[1]

Something else comes before mission and service: love for
the Lord 'who loved me and gave himself for me' (Gal
2:20). When love for Christ is at the centre, mission and
service will flow out of that centre without any need for us
to worry too much about it. Our activities, and any impact
we may have, will be as a reply, a response to God's love
for us, as if our lives were an echo chamber for his love.
But we must not love him as a means to an end, or because
'when Christians love, things happen', or 'when congregations love, churches grow'. This would be a calculating use
of love, where 'blessing' or 'growth' become idols.

Love seeks nothing but love in return. God has given
himself to us in love, and he desires nothing but our love
in return. Love for God, sincere and without strings, is the
one true measure of the Christian life.

What is my clout as a Christian? What do I amount to?
Augustine put it succinctly: 'My weight is my love'. Of
course, we love the blessings, the gifts and the benefits
which God's love brings us. We need intensely to feel his
love: it gives us inexpressible joy and a taste of glory to
come (1 Peter 1:8). 'I do love thee! And when I love thee
not chaos is come again' was Othello's famous description
of how it is for people in love. But deliverance from chaos
is an effect of love, not the reason for loving. We must practice the art of loving God's love with no ulterior motives.

Love for love's sake

Have you noticed what is missing in the Song of Songs?
The two lovers – bride and bridegroom – are childless. The

couple are together in the enclosed garden of their mutual love, and there are no children. Thus it is with Christ and his church. The Lord wants first our faithful love. He has not called us so as to get something from us, but because he loves us and desires our sincere love in return.

I recall my sense of relief when listening to a well-known evangelist talk about his attitude to service. He said, 'When my son was born, I didn't go straight round to the newsagents and put his name down for a paper round!' Neither does the Lord think of us primarily as so many workers for his projects. (If he did, he would surely make it easier for us to get our hands on those projects!) He calls us because he loves us, without ulterior motives, a fact which we seem to find very difficult to accept. But it is true: love comes before mission and makes our witness authentically Christian.

> Awake, north wind,
>   and come, south wind!
> Blow on my garden,
>   that its fragrance may spread abroad.
>   *(Song of Songs 4:16)*

This beautiful and suggestive image portrays faith-sharing as the overflow of love, and witness as a fragrant quality carried around on the breath of the Holy Spirit. The saints have always known that Christlike mission comes to birth in this way – not by looking at the task but by looking at him: 'Love leads to meditation, which leads to contemplation, which leads to jubilation, which leads to compassion' (Richard of Chichester). When we go to meet Jesus in his word, as we listen to him, he will appear in our hearts. The effect will be joy and delight at the sight of him, and we will find ourselves looking at the world through the eyes of his compassion. The saints are first and foremost people who constantly give thanks for having been loved, and who cannot forget the misery of once not having loved or let Christ love them.

We serve God's love – that is our highest priority every time. To a busy world engaged in so many big projects, the priority of love will appear irrelevant, even self-indulgent. Thus when Mary poured her costly perfume over Jesus' feet and wiped them with her hair, her extravagant act of devotion provoked a business-like and pragmatic objection: surely the needs of the poor should come before expressions of devotion to Christ (John 12:1–5). Judas was not to know that, in fact, immense movements of Christian compassion and practical love would flow from people energised by love for Christ: 'You gave so much for me, what can I give to thee?' (Zinzendorf).

For the same reason, we must side with Mary who 'sat at the Lord's feet listening to what he said' while Martha was 'distracted by all the preparations' (Luke 10:38–42). We may find this, and Jesus' support for Mary's decision, irksome: 'It's all very well, but there's work to be done. Heaven help us if the world is ever left for Marys to run!' But notice the events which lead up to that episode. Jesus had sent out the seventy-two evangelists to engage in prophetic proclamation, with the signs and wonders of powerful exorcisms (vs 1–24). This is followed by that great parable of Christlike love in action, the Good Samaritan (vs 25–37). These two passages are at the heart of New Testament missionary vision, yet they lead to the extraordinary conclusion in that small village home: 'only one thing is needed. Mary has chosen what is better' (v 42).

Of course, our Lord is not setting Mary against Martha: rather, he is establishing the proper order of Christian mission. First Mary's attitude, and then Martha's service. Love Christ, and service will follow. Love, and trust love to overflow in creative Christlike behaviour. But no one who does not know the Lord in meditation and contemplation will recognise him as he acts in the world. Only sitting 'at the Lord's feet listening to what he says' can save us from the delusions that masquerade as love.

> There is a love which is without love, a self-surrender which is not surrender, a paroxysm of self-love which has the external appearance of an authentic love of God and our brother, the love which will go to the ultimate limits of self-surrender, but which is in reality not at all concerned with God and our brother ... Only love itself counts; no acts of love as such, not even the greatest (1 Cor 13:1–3). These can also be done without love and they are then meaningless. Even worse – they are often done against God and our brother!
>
> *(Karl Barth)*[2]

Do you love me?

Genuine love is unaware of itself; it does not constantly watch itself to see how it is doing; it has no deliberate intention. Only love can be free from self and genuinely available to others. First love, then mission; first Mary, then Martha; first the Lord, then his service.

> The arrogant person is like a black object. In order to acquire some energy and thus be able to 'shine' he sucks up all light into himself, not knowing that precisely because of this he no longer reflects a single ray and so is wholly darkness. The humble person is already bright: whatever he receives he passes on, and he shines precisely because he does not clutch at things. Because he readily transmits the borrowed light that falls on him, he himself becomes light.
>
> *(Balthasar)*[3]

Love and mission are one; Mary and Martha are one; love and spiritual impact are one.

> To help another person come to love God is to love him; and to be supported by another person in loving God is to be loved.
>
> *(Søren Kierkegaard)*

For the Christian who loves the Lord first, terms like 'barrenness', 'ineffectiveness', 'fruitlessness' and 'uselessness' do not apply.

At the heart of God's engagement with his people is the one question, 'Do you love me?' Not, 'Are you effective/powerful/impressive?' Just 'Do you love me?' Love is the only service that power cannot command nor money buy. Duty makes us do things well but love makes us do them beautifully. Mother Teresa would call upon her sisters to go with her into the streets of Calcutta and 'do something beautiful for God' – with love and care, to the best of our gifts and abilities.

When things are done for the love of God, any cost or sacrifice incurred must be kept secret: 'when you fast, put oil on your head and wash your face, so that it will not be obvious to men that you are fasting' (Matt 6:16–18). If I should buy a present for my wife and then publish in the church magazine how much I paid for it, we would soon be heading for the divorce courts! Ostentation negates the gift. Only the Lord must know how much our love for him is costing us. In the Holy Spirit, we have an inner, personal and secret life with God, who sees what we intend and is glad to receive whatever we mean for him in love.

Friends were visiting us from the US and we were soon catching up on news and talking about old times. Our conversation turned to two men who had had a profound effect upon us. Both had been scientists at the Admiralty, but left to become schoolteachers with the aim of starting Christian youth work in that part of London. They immersed themselves in their vision with a painstaking thoroughness that led to a stream of young people coming to faith in Christ. We recalled the sheer sustained quality of their service, which only a few people ever realised.

On another occasion, while out with those same friends, we visited some of the lovely Rutland villages. We went into the small church of St Peter, Tickencote, having heard that the chancel was well worth seeing. We were quite unprepared for the breathtaking beauty of the quintuple Norman chancel. The five arches – each carved with highly individualistic designs and meeting together to form a single arch – were carved around 1150. Whatever one's taste in these things, some unknown craftsmen had lavished extraordinary skill and love on this astonishing work in a little stone building in the forest. Not in a great cathedral, where a mason's reputation could be made; but in Tickencote, 'a name from the Saxon ticcen and cote', meaning 'the place where goats and kids were herded in the forest', an unimportant place in a remote spot. There, virtually in secret, men had expressed their love for God. Nine hundred years later, the spiritual impact of their love is awesome. A sure sign of genuine love and reverence is secrecy, which humbly conceals the motives of our actions.

Chapter 11

SLOW GOLD

I would like to salute the Swiss Tourist Board for their honest advertising. Switzerland is the one place I know where the real thing is, if anything, even lovelier than it is painted in the brochures. I am not sure that in the church we are as transparent. Are we telling each other the whole truth about the way we experience the power of God? I suspect we are more like the Albanian Tourist Board, selective with our pictures and slanted with our reports. And it is not difficult to see why.

Christians strive for relevance. Of course we do. Unless people around us can perceive the gospel as impinging on their real concerns, there will be no communication. We may preach, but no one will stay around long enough to listen. Thus the demand 'to be relevant' pulls on the way we present the Christian faith. Naturally, we favour those aspects of the message which appeal to society and, naturally, we tend to play down its more enigmatic, mysterious and disturbing dimensions. But 'relevance' is a slippery word. Newman warned against what he called 'shedding the riches and vitality of actual experience in order to promote artificial clarity'. It is a mistake to dumb down the gospel for the sake of a dubious 'relevance'.

How extraordinary it is that believers who are struggling to live effectively in today's world should, over and over again, turn back to the drama of Job. From Latin

America, Elsa Tamez writes this startling tribute to the relevance of the 'irrelevant' Job:[1]

> The smell of death that is about you reaches our nostrils;
> we smell you everywhere. Your skeletal body goads us.
> Shreds of your corroding flesh hang from our flesh; you
> have infected us, brother Job, you have infected us, our
> families, our people. And your look of one who thirsts for
> justice and your breath that is soaked in wrath have
> filled us with courage, tenderness and hope.

Job's story is not for the squeamish. He disturbs our theories about how God moves in human experience. He is often a repellent figure, but he fulfils Simone Weil's maxim that 'to be always relevant you have to say things that are eternal'.

Job is the ancient soul-friend of the oppressed, particularly those who persist with God even while blaming him for their troubles, who 'flee from God to God'. In Job's story, the Holy Spirit has poured wisdom and light for our own confused times, and has given us divine permission to be as honest about our own faith journey as Job was with his. 'Personal troubles, followed by slow healing in the face of much misunderstanding' – this is Job's experience, and it is often ours. We hear of committed Christians passing through deep and disabling times, and we call this their 'Job experience'.

David, a well-read and deeply committed evangelical in Glasgow, describes his 'Job' time:

> In Pat Barker's *Regeneration*, two approaches to the
> recovery of soldiers traumatised by trench warfare are
> brought into sharp focus. W H Rivers, an army
> psychologist, practices the art of caring, confidential,
> attentive, empathic, patient listening. He refuses to rush

the recuperative process. Progress is painfully slow but 'gentle miracles' do, unspectacularly, emerge. In contrast, there is the sheer, intimidating, overwhelming power of Dr Yealland's electrical room. Here, things move much faster. Patients may not leave until cured. The results are undeniably impressive. The mute speak, and remember to give thanks to their omnipotent healer.

When, in December 1992, five years into paid Christian ministry, I was signed off work with depression, my main hope was for a speedy recovery. It never materialised. God seemed stubbornly, unreasonably, unyieldingly resistant to all my bugle calls summoning the divine seventh cavalry over the brow of the hill. Instead, progress was slow, tentative, partial, often imperceptible. The healing agencies? A sympathetic, unobtrusive employer who allowed me time and space to mend. The hospitality (in the richest biblical sense) of a kind family providing a safe place to recuperate. A lengthy process of dismantling and rebuilding with a wise, common-sense, down-to-earth counsellor whose approach was more comprehensive and thorough than anything else I have encountered in the Christian market-place, and who refused to be deflected by the short-cut, quick-fix solutions I consistently flagged up. The support and encouragement of accepting friends who took me as they found me. Reading which illuminated something of what I was feeling in the dark: Dostoevsky's vulnerable Christlike Prince Myshkin in *The Idiot*; Walter Brueggemann's writing on Israel's prophet-poets of the exile; Henri Nouwen's analysis of the resentful elder son of Jesus' parable; Harry William's exploration of the false view of God in *The True Wilderness* (sadly, there is little of any of this in the public teaching ministry of the church, where, all too often, slogans that are inadequate to the facts of our existence predominate).

What has changed for me five years on? Perspectives have fairly radically altered, though, like Jacob, I am left limping, marked by the experience. I hope I can say that I am a great deal less 'spiritual' and a good deal more human, that there is a bit more congruence between the public presentation and the private reality. Why does healing take so long? Something to do with elastoplasts being insufficient when radical surgery is required. Martin Israel writes, 'On the whole, a slow, deliberate type of healing is ultimately more beneficial than a sudden, dramatic one. A sudden cure is liable to concentrate the whole attention on the body or the mind, depending on the nature of the illness. A slower return to health provides the sick person with more time to deliberate on his life's course, and to treat the healing he is receiving with sober reverence. That which comes to us far too easily seldom makes its impact permanently felt in the personality; after the initial rejoicing, it tends to be taken for granted and forgotten.'

Many of us will have passed through something similar, and these experiences share certain features: a busy life disrupted by set-backs (ill-health, depression, loss or failure), followed by bewilderment and a crisis of faith disillusionment at what seems like superficial 'Christian' answers; then deliverance and restoration, emerging into new wisdom and usefulness. This process, however painful, is an instance of Newman's 'richness and vitality of actual experience', although it is hardly marketable stuff in a culture so obsessed with quick-fix solutions. To be relevant in such a culture, so impressed by image, style and spin, we are severely tempted to deal in short-cut solutions and slogans that are 'inadequate to the facts of our existence'. Rather, let us contemplate Job's predicament.

God and Satan have a wager: 'Does Job fear God for nothing?' challenges Satan (Job 1:9), implying that Job's commitment to God is very much for his own benefit (v 10). A student of human nature, Satan has toured the world, observing human motivation and behaviour. He is convinced that the whole lot of us are out for our own ends. If we worship God at all, it is at best cupboard love: we want God's goods more than we want God himself.

Whatever else he might be, Satan knows his theology. He understands full well what will pull the linchpin out of the created order: without love for God, nothing can stand; the reason for our existence (the perichoresis discussed in chapter 9) would disintegrate. Our beautiful liturgies and exuberant praise-gatherings, our sacrificial service, do not impress the cynical principalities and powers one bit. They are sure it is all driven by self-interest. Yet God insists that in Job he has a representative human being who adores God for himself and not out of ulterior motives (v 8).

Job, of course, has no idea of the cosmic drama buzzing around him. It is a disturbing thought that we could, unknowingly, be the ones who carry God's reputation where we live or work. In the end, it will be the quality of our love for the Lord which validates the gospel before the watching heavenly powers, not the excellence of our arguments which can always be trumped. Job is put to the test without knowing the reason for what is happening to him. Out of a clear blue sky, his life is laid in ruins. He loses his possessions and wealth, his family and finally his health.

The lament
There is a logic to the prayers of lament found in scripture, and it is that everything which touches us touches God. The darkest experiences are reckoned proper subjects

for conversation with him. When Job articulates his hurt and confusion, he is bringing everything into God's domain: 'After this, Job opened his mouth and cursed the day of his birth ... "Why is life given to a man whose way is hidden, whom God has hedged in?"' (3:1,23). Job believes that nothing in his life is out of bounds to God. The alternative is for us to do what we do most of the time – to split our inner life between the sunny, happy, upbeat and praiseworthy, and the chaotic, painful concerns which we mutter to ourselves in the dark.

Walter Brueggemann describes the lament as being able to evoke reality for someone who has engaged in self-deception and who still imagines that life is well-ordered when in fact it is not. For Brueggemann, laments like Job's (and those in the Psalms and elsewhere) are 'statements of disorientation':[2]

> The harsh and abrasive speech of a statement of disorientation may penetrate the deception and say, 'No, this is how it really is.' In such a case language leads experience so that the speaker speaks what is unknown and inexperienced until it is finally brought to speech. It is not this way until it is said to be this way.
>
> It is no wonder that the Church has intuitively avoided these Psalms [of lament]. They lead us into dangerous acknowledgement of how life really is. They lead us into the presence of God where everything is not polite and civil. They cause us to think unthinkable thoughts and utter unutterable words. Perhaps worst, they lead us away from the conformable religious claims of modernity in which everything is managed and controlled.
>
> In our modern experience, but probably also in every successful and affluent culture, it is believed that enough power and knowledge can tame the terror and eliminate

the darkness. Very much a religion of orientation operates on that basis. But our honest experience, both personal and public, attests to the resilience of the darkness in spite of us. The remarkable thing about Israel is that it did not banish or deny darkness from its religious enterprise. It embraces the darkness as the very stuff of new life. Indeed, Israel seems to know that new life comes nowhere else.

We have divine permission to stand in God's presence with our heart-break. Jesus did. 'My God, my God, why have you forsaken me?' (Matt 27:46). But the Lord will not leave us lamenting. Job (in anticipation of Jesus) will go through darkness into light, through disorientation into a new orientation, through death into resurrection – many times over. The result is, said Emily Dickinson, like gold, 'slow gold – but everlasting'.

The friends
Job is a ghastly sight with a repellent skin condition, quarantined on his ash heap. Under the stress of his illness and grief, he desperately needs friends. Friends were crucial to David in Glasgow, and to the lady who wrote the following:

> Life has narrowed further and medication is causing problems ... a feature of my health is the sudden ups and downs, constant readjusting of horizon, and I mentioned to a Christian friend a couple of days ago that to me it feels like 'brainwashing' which leads to confusion and weariness.

She goes on to mention the support that friends are giving her.

Job's famous three friends may not be wise or very

cheerful, but they certainly 'mean well' (Job 2:11–13), a phrase to send shudders down the spine. To analyse their efforts, let us look at them alongside Martin Luther's 'remedies for depression':

- Avoid being alone.

Isolation is poison for the depressed person, for through this the devil attempts to keep him in his power. 'Talk among ourselves, so that I know I am surrounded by other people,' said Luther one day, when feeling depressed.

Job's friends come close and sit 'on the ground with him for seven days and seven nights'.

- Seek out people or situations which generate joy.

Joy is always pleasing to God, even though it may not be of a strictly religious origin.

No joy for poor Job. His friends hold to the traditional line that he is suffering on account of sin in his life or in the life of his family (ch 4).

- Sing and make music!

- Dismiss heavy thoughts.

Beware of becoming engrossed by gloomy despairing thoughts. Laugh at the devil or scorn him, but by no means give in to him.

Job's friends pile on the agony!

- Rely upon the promises of scripture.

They encourage our minds to think positively, especially verses learned by heart.

- Seek consolation from others.

When depressed, we often make mountains out of molehills. A friend sees things in the right perspective and reminds us of the realities to which we are momentarily blind.

Unfortunately, Job does not have a Luther among his friends! They deal in dogma instead. They insist on the tight connection between sin and suffering, merit and prosperity. Bad things happen to bad people, good things come to good people.

Job rejects his friends' analysis: the old view simply does not cover the facts of his desolating experiences. He is innocent, yet God allows him to suffer. At this point it is interesting to return to David's letter and note his reaction to the 'answers' he encountered in the churches, the 'short-cut, quick-fix solutions', 'slogans that are inadequate to the facts of our existence'. There exists too great a discrepancy between what people find in their Monday-to-Saturday life, and what they hear in church.

The answer

When God at last answers Job, he shows him creation. He parades the cosmos past Job, allowing it to speak for him. All God does is to fire off a stream of counter-question: 'Do you know? Were you there? Can you tell?'

> All things therefore are charged with love, are charged with God and if we know how to touch them give off sparks and take fire, yield drops and flow, ring and tell of him.
>
> *(Hopkins)*[3]

As the parable of creation dances before Job, it triggers the realisation that he has been wrong all along about God (42:1–3). Yet this is not the only reason for his utter self-abasement: 'Therefore I despise myself and repent in dust and ashes' (v 6). Something more than acknowledgement of error and submission to God's superior power and intelligence is in that cry. Job offers no reasons or deductions, only his gasp of recognition: 'My ears had heard of you but now my eyes have seen you' (v 5). Something happens to him in that strange moment of disclosure, which overwhelms his mind. Whatever it is, however it breaks in upon him, it resolves his difficulties with God instantaneously and sets them in a wholly new light, relieving his exhausted mind. The 'problem of suffering' is not solved as such, but rather it ceases to be so all-consuming:

> Seeing God, Job forgets all he wanted to say, all he thought he would say if he could but see him.
>
> *(George MacDonald)*[4]

Face to face with God, Job realises that God is himself the only 'answer' that can satisfy us in the mystery of undeserved suffering. God never answers Job's problem, but the problem becomes more luminous as Job's vision of God expands. At the end, the solution of the plot is not the solution of the problem. Only the revelation of Christ's redemptive suffering on the cross can interpret God's mysterious ways with us.

> When a composer such as God creates the opera of the world and places in its centre his crucified and risen Son, every fault-finding at his work – ie whether or not he could have done it better – must be reduced to silence.
>
> *(Balthasar)*[5]

Chapter 12

THE HUMILIATED FOOL

Are Christians fools? Yes, in that love for Jesus can inspire normal, healthy people to cheerfully give themselves over to an uncomfortable existence.

'We are fools for Christ' (1 Cor 4:10) in the estimation of unbelievers who wonder why anyone would want to take their religion so seriously. 'Worship, if it makes you happy. Pray, if you must. But whatever you do, on no account imagine that your religion makes any difference.' We are fools if we allow faith in Jesus to touch our purse; to interfere with our leisure, pleasure and relationships; to turn the other cheek; to overlook debts; to walk the second mile; even to lower our standard of living. If to exchange comfort for hardship is foolishness then, yes, Christians are fools.

Daniel Mpembele became a Christian at a Scripture Union camp in Zaire, when he fled there to escape the civil war in Angola. Back in Luanda, he faced suspicion when he gave up a secure job as a meteorologist and became the driving force behind SU Angola's Bible reading ministry. Why was the man throwing away relative comfort and security to risk his future in such tenuous work? No wonder the nervous authorities were suspicious, just as we all are uncertain in the presence of unusual behaviour. Yet Pauline Hoggarth wrote of him, 'Our conference ... was lit up by Daniel's singing and laughter.'

A Russian Christian, Gregory Petrov, accepted exile in one of Stalin's Siberian labour camps rather than deny Christ. Before he died in the 1940s, he wrote his ecstatic 'Akathist of Thanksgiving' – a hymn 'giving glory to God for everything':[1]

> Glory to you, who has shown us the light,
> Glory to you, loving us with a love
> Deep, immeasurable divine,
> Glory to you, enlightening us with light,
> With the host of angels and saints,
> Glory to you, all-holy Father,
> Who has given us charge of your kingdom,
> Glory to you, Holy Spirit,
> Life-giving sun of the ages to come,
> Glory to you for everything,
> All-gracious Trinity divine ...
> Life's tempests hold no dread
> For him in whose heart shines the lamp of your fire.
> All around, foul weather and gloom,
> Horror and wailing of wind,
> But, in his soul, serenity and light.
> Christ is there! And the heart sings: Alleluia.

To the unbelieving observer this appears fanatical, a sort of lunacy. A man stands in the terrible Siberian cold and cries out, 'Christ is there! And the heart sings: Alleluia.' But in his hymn, Petrov includes a verse which describes his conversion experience, when the living Christ over-whelmed his mind:

> As when after lightning has lit up
> The banqueting chamber,
> The lights seem faint from the lamps,
> So you of a sudden blazed in my soul

At times of intense worldly pleasures.
And after the lightning flash of your light,
How colourless, dark,
What illusions they seemed!

A high-flying Swiss nurse stepped off the career ladder to come to England and learn the language en route to medical work in the developing world. Her family and nursing superiors in Switzerland tried hard to dissuade her from 'throwing away her future' in some remote corner of Asia. But, in her early days in Leeds, a confirmation was given her by God, when she befriended a woman dying of cancer. Although she had only limited English, she was able to read part of John's Gospel to the sick woman and to help her to faith in Christ before she died. Was our Swiss nurse a fool?

In Latin America, Fr Joao-Bosco Burnier was murdered at a police station, where he had gone to protest the mistreatment of two women. Bishop Pedro Casaldaliga, who went with him, writes:[2]

He died for justice and charity. In Amazonia. At an especially critical time, a time of martyrs ... Pray that we may be faithful, that the Spirit will keep giving us the gift of joy, that the church may bear witness to the very end ... The Lord is the resurrection and the life. And the communion of the entire church is with us. And this death and these threats serve as a witness to others, 'outside', who are also struggling for the new humankind. This is not a sad time, but a beautiful gospel time.

In a culture like our own, obsessed with length and quality of life, to call a good man's violent murder 'a beautiful gospel time' sounds bizarre and possibly deranged. Was Fr Burnier a fool?

Fantasy at Corinth

The Christians at Corinth did not fancy being anyone's fool. They evolved a very attractive slant on life – 'Everything is permissible for me' (1 Cor 6:12) – a view that emphasised their rights of immediate possession. All things are Christ's and we are in him, hence all things are ours. Christ is throwing a fabulous party: show your appreciation by enjoying everything on offer. And Paul agrees (3:21–23). However, as often happens with spiritual perception, the Corinthians had become mesmerised by one aspect of the truth and would allow nothing to moderate it. They were right about the riches we have in Christ, but disastrously wrong about the nature of life in the kingdom this side of Christ's Second Coming. Their view gave the Corinthians a crown without a cross, splendour without conflict. The key word in their idea of the Christian life was 'already' with no thought of 'not yet' (4:8). Paul's ironic comment? 'Already' they have eaten their fill, they are sated, they have it all, they deny themselves nothing; 'already' they are enjoying their riches, they have come into their kingdom. They behave as if the age to come had come already, and already the saints had climbed onto their thrones and taken over the kingdom. There is no room in such an understanding for the costliness of living in the world as Christ's fools.

The truth is that for the present we live in the tension between 'already' and 'not yet' (sometimes called 'living in the overlap'). Christ the King has triumphed by his cross and resurrection, but as yet his kingdom is not revealed to the universe. It is there, but concealed behind the curtain, awaiting the Father's signal for it to be manifested to an astounded creation. For the present, Christians are in the world as the King's children who live as fools for Christ. Paul agrees with the Corinthians: it would be a marvellous thing if they were right, and the apostles and the saints did now reign as kings. As it is, we still pray for God's kingdom to come, for what is hidden to be revealed. Now we live by faith, not by sight. The end has not yet arrived (15:24); the time for fulfilment and prosperity is not here.

> This life is not health, but healing; not being, but becoming; not rest, but exercise. We are not yet what we shall be, but we are growing toward it; the process is not yet finished, but it is going on; this is not the end, but it is the road. All does not yet gleam in glory, but all is being purified.
>
> *(Martin Luther)*

The tension between 'already' and 'not yet' gives the Christian a distinctive stance in relation to the world: triumphant and joyful, but tough and demanding. Paul proceeds to paint a picture of authentic discipleship (4:9–13). While the Corinthians pursue their 'victorious' lives in which spiritual blessings fuel self-esteem, the apostles embrace the consequences of their love for Christ in a hostile world. Very far from enjoying 'all things', Paul feels like those wretched prisoners brought out at the end of the day's entertainment in the arena, men who are marked out for death (v 9). The arena is the world; the spectators are all heaven and earth; the apostles are the spectacle of weakness and humiliation.

The Corinthians imagine that their 'superior' approach to the Christian life puts them in the position of enlightenment, but they have sanitised the gospel by their sophistication. They have made respectable the terrible cross.

> Jesus did not die just any death; he was 'given up for us all' on the cross, in a cruel and a contemptible way ...

Jesus did not die a gentle death like Socrates, with his cup of hemlock, much less passing on 'old and full of years' like the patriarchs of the Old Testament. Rather, he died like a slave or a common criminal, on a tree of shame.

(Martin Hengel)[3]

We follow Christ in the face of opposition. The world being what it is, genuine Christian witness will be opposed.

Our century has seen more concentrated hatred of God than any other ... the denigration of God, the ridiculing of belief in him ... has become a potent force in our civilisation, and it often has the power to paralyse Christian vigour and praise.

(Daniel Hardy)[4]

Paul outlines the apostles' struggles (4:10–13): the dangers, the insults, the hardship; 'we go hungry and thirsty, we are in rags, we are brutally treated, we are homeless' (v 11); 'we have become the scum of the earth, the refuse of the world' (v 13), scrapings, off-scouring, useless waste. The word translated 'scum' also carries the meaning of 'scapegoat', which suggests the double idea of a person who is despised and driven-away yet who serves a vicarious function for the community.

Two conceptions of ministry are compared in those verses. The Corinthian one ('already you have become rich') and the apostolic one ('We are fools for Christ'). To the 'wise' Corinthians, Paul is 'a fool' to suffer as he has, and a humiliating embarrassment to their spiritually high-flying church. But there is no doubt which conception of ministry corresponds more closely to the Lord's command: 'If anyone would come after me, he must deny himself and take up his cross and follow me' (Mark 8:34). Suffering is part of the service of a messenger. The world's resentment must be expected: hate is a common response to witness and testimony. And here lies the paradox: through the 'weakness and folly of the cross', the church thrives.

> Let us never forget that in its first and mightiest conflict against the powers of this world represented in the imperial might of Rome, the victory of the Gospel was won not by the cleverness of its preachers and theologians, and certainly not by its programmes of social justice but by the blood of the martyrs ... in the USSR ... in China ... In Latin America where the blood of countless martyrs has been shed in witness to the Gospel against the cruel and unjust dictatorship.
>
> *(Lesslie Newbigin)*[5]

Take up your cross

Newbigin's words affirm the ancient wisdom that 'the blood of the martyrs is the seed of the church'. Yet Jesus' command that we 'take up our cross' and follow him does not refer primarily to martyrdom: as the wording in Luke 9:23 shows, we are to take up our cross daily and follow him. A particular moment is imagined in our Lord's words: the beginning of the walk to the place of execution, when the condemned prisoner takes the patibulum, the beam of the cross, on his shoulder and steps out of the judgement room into the dazzling Mediterranean sunlight, to face the jeering hostile mob. This is the first test, even before the moment of crucifixion, when the prisoner must push through the crowds, an outcast, utterly alone, helpless to defend himself against their contempt and mockery. A rabbinical saying runs, 'Come and hear ... anyone who ... strikes a man who is being led out to execution ... is free of punishment ... for the victim counts as a dead man.' To be Christ's fool means to embark on a life that may be as hard for us as Christ's last walk was for him.

The hard walk of the way of the cross applies to everyone, not just to the apostles nor to other luminaries in the church ('if anyone would come after me', Mark 8:34). And following Jesus involves the likelihood of walking the lonely road through people's hostility. In subsequent chapters, we will explore how it is that the exposed weakness of walking Christ's walk makes us strong and effective, 'weak enough for God to use'.

Chapter 13

JARS, THORNS AND POWER

The art of living lies in getting the better of our weaknesses and difficulties. Weakness is negative, power is positive. Christians go along with that sort of reckoning because, obviously, it is how life works: so obvious, in fact, that we make it our chief line of evangelistic appeal – Jesus Christ is the true source of real power. Only believe and connect.

Yes and no. Yes, Jesus is certainly all those things and more; but no, he does not give a straight swap between our weaknesses and his victory, like trading in an old, broken washing machine for a brand new one. Some preachers say that he does, but they are promising too much and sow the seeds of future disillusionment. Or, rather, they do not promise enough, or show how Jesus bestows his power on us by harnessing our flawed personalities and drawing us deeper into his life.

Of all people, the apostle Paul was pre-eminently qualified to speak of spiritual power and effectiveness, of victory and growth. His achievements were phenomenal. He planted and established the first Christian churches, and has influenced billions of Christians down the ages through his writings. Yet he quite bluntly told the young churches that they 'must go through many hardships to enter the kingdom of God'. In his view, such trials would strengthen the disciples and encourage them 'to remain true to the faith' (Acts 14:21–22). To the Corinthians he was, if anything, even more forthright about the place of suffering in the life of the Spirit-led Christian. Three times in his second letter to them, he lists his own severe experiences (2 Cor 4:7–11; 6:4–10; 11:22–29) to authenticate his apostolic ministry. God had placed him not on a pedestal but next to the powerlessness of the cross (13:4). He declares:

> I will boast all the more gladly about my weaknesses, so that Christ's power may rest on me. That is why, for Christ's sake, I delight in weaknesses, in insults, in hardships, in persecutions, in difficulties. For when I am weak, then I am strong.
>
> *(2 Corinthians 12:9–10)*

This may seem like strange talk to our modern ears. We do not usually embrace our troubles so. We equate success with obvious results. We are more in tune with attitudes like that of the pastor of a mega-church in Florida (congregation 7,000), who explained his success thus: 'I must be doing right, or things wouldn't be going so well'. This attitude is more akin to that of a captain of industry addressing the shareholders at the end of a good year! However, Paul's words suggest that no statistics can encompass God's secret work in the lives of his people.

At a gathering of Anglican evangelists working in the north of England, we were listening to a presentation of ideas for church growth. One of our group quietly made the observation, 'But it's much more mysterious than that, isn't it?' Working in a tough inner-city parish in the North East, he had tried the usual strategies and ideas, with little success. He did not know how to reach the local people, but decided to keep the church open for prayer each day. Then, quite inexplicably, numbers of young people started coming into the church after school for a simple service – not for games, videos and food, but for the service. He was right, these things are mysterious. It is another instance of Christ in his power coming to rest on a place of 'wit's-end' despair and weakness.

An entrance for power

Paul embraced things we would regard as obstacles to our desire to live for God. Yet he was not a masochist in love with pain, or an ascetic who rejects comfort in pursuit of soul-making. He was not a Gnostic who despises this-world life, or a Buddhist who regards physical existence as illusion. Quite simply, he was a full-blooded Jew who became totally Christ-struck: 'For to me, to live is Christ ... I consider everything a loss compared to the surpassing greatness of knowing Christ Jesus my Lord, for whose sake I have lost all things' (Phil 1:21; 3:8). His love for Christ is the clue to his attitude regarding the place of weakness in the believer's life. For him, Christ's redeeming grace, flowing to us from his cross and resurrection, is the most stupendous and dazzlingly beautiful power in the universe. An irresistible logic follows from that truth -- that each person, if they are to be a real human being before God, should receive Christ in all the riches of his grace.

But Jesus taught us to be realistic: 'It is not the healthy who need a doctor, but the sick' (Matt 9:12). It is simply a fact: human weakness provides the opportunity for divine power to enter and work. Therefore, Paul reasons, any experience or circumstance which provokes people to call for the doctor is priceless. When we imagine ourselves secure within our prosperity, we lose any sense of urgency. We have no strong incentive to cry out to Christ. We are 'healthy' and in no need of the doctor. The 'sick', however, are beyond pretending. They need help and admit as much.

Then faith is simplified. Flowery prayers become a short gasp of desire for God. Apparently sophisticated attitudes become primitive and immediate. If conditions of weakness or hardship can break down our apathy and pride, Paul reasons, let us by all means value weakness and hardship when they appear in our lives, for they prepare a way for the Lord.

This is a clue to why churches in poorer countries often seem so much more vital and joyful, more open-hearted and faster growing than those in richer countries. A group of young Baptist volunteers from the UK, who were working in India, appeared on BBC Television. Their work with clinics and children had impressed them deeply. There were two things in particular: the precariousness of life for people in the slums, and the radiant faith and joy of local Christians. One of the group remarked, 'They (the local Christians) live their Christian lives in the open for everyone to see, seven days a week – not like us at home!' Christians who habitually depend on the Lord seem blessed with a depth of reality and joy.

Therefore, Paul says, 'I will boast all the more gladly about my weaknesses, so that Christ's power may rest on me ... For when I am weak, then I am strong.' For him, weaknesses were not destructive of his ministry but essential to it. Knowing that the strong presence of Christ was with him in his difficulties qualified him to be an authentic witness to Christ's power.

Jesus is the same Lord and Saviour in Calcutta as in Henley-upon-Thames. The problem for the latter is that its prosperous secularism creates the myth of self-sufficiency, the illusion of autonomy, that we are self-making and self-sustaining people. The effect is to create a sort of soft, practical atheism which dilutes our sense of need for Christ's intervention. The concept of the dynamic grace of God thus appears dreamy, thin, remote and unreal. In the fourth century, the great preacher Chrysostom noticed the same process in his churches:

> How great is the advantage of affliction; for now indeed we are supine and lax, and have filled the church with countless evils; but when we were persecuted we were more sober-minded and more earnest and more ready for church attendance and for learning.

Life out of death

When Christ found room to move in Paul's life through his hardships, some profoundly Christlike effects followed: 'known, yet regarded as unknown; dying, and yet we live on; beaten, and yet not killed; sorrowful, yet always rejoicing; poor, yet making many rich; having nothing, and yet possessing everything' (2 Cor 6:9–10). This is how Christ's 'fools' interpret their difficulties and weaknesses – not cursing their troubles, but allowing Christ, in his love and power, to take them up and transmute them into blessing.

> In this you greatly rejoice, though now for a little while you may have had to suffer grief in all kinds of trials. These have come so that your faith – of greater worth than gold, which perishes even though refined by fire – may be proved genuine and may result in praise, glory and honour when Jesus Christ is revealed.
>
> *(1 Peter 1:6–7)*

It is hard to attain such rich depths of spirituality when we are living in our complacent ease and plenty which more often render us 'supine and lax'. No one in their right mind goes looking for hard times, nor is there any need to. Life, our experience of 'the world, the flesh, and the devil', our own fallen natures and that of our fellow human beings, will see to it that there are constant opportunities for Christ to enter our affairs and do his work. As he does so, we will reach new levels of maturity. We will have a testimony, we will be witnesses, when we prove the paradox in ourselves: 'I delight in weaknesses ... For when I am weak, then I am strong'.

An artist, a woman of deep Christian faith, wrote to us about her own experience of this paradox. She and her husband suffered the appalling loss of their son and his wife in a car accident several years ago. Then her husband died suddenly in the midst of a busy and fruitful ministry.

I was numbed, overwhelmed with the unbelievable loss. The thought of living alone and managing house, garden, van, money, boiler and letters seemed impossible without him. One day I cried out, 'But I can't ask David any more!' Immediately came an almost audible voice. 'Ask me,' said the Lord, so I did. Every half hour I asked him about everything, silly ordinary things as well as more important. I asked all the time, 'What do I do next, Lord?' I would do the first things that came to mind. I found it necessary to obey, and it was amazing how things worked out. I was able to accomplish so much that I thought I could never do. The day was ordered. I wrote lists, but only did things when the Spirit told me to do them. I had unexpected encounters, advice at the right time. I was led to a new car, a lovely holiday with new friends, booked only just in time. I was helped to overcome fears of going out and travelling alone. Car park spaces became available when I prayed for them. I am still having to learn to ask and obey, especially how to ask for right thoughts and attitudes towards life and others, to pray against their fears and negative beliefs, as well as my own. I do thank God for his presence and his blessings and, most of all, for his promises of eternal life, where and when we shall be united with our dear ones.

Paul stressed the contrast between what we are when left to ourselves and what we become when the grace of God in Christ comes upon our naturalness. We are inclined to absorb and assimilate the power of Christ as if it were naturally our own. Paul will have none of this: the glory belongs to God alone. That is the theme of his second letter to the Corinthians.

'Treasure in jars of clay'

A dramatic contrast: priceless jewels in a plain, cheap jar (2 Cor 4:6–12). The dazzling brilliance and the value of the treasure are intensified when set against the ordinary container.

Paul's critics mocked him because 'in person he is unimpressive and his speaking amounts to nothing' (10:10). By implication, if the messenger is not easy on the eye or the ear, his message will be equally unimpressive. Nonsense, says Paul, can't you see the distinction? The message of 'the light ... of the glory of God in the face of Christ' (4:6) is not the product of our minds. There are two entities here – the treasure, and the container which God has, amazingly, decided should hold it. Our shortcomings present no barrier to his purposes. Indeed, God's power is 'made perfect in weakness' (12:9) and transcends ordinary limits.

A minister gives the following account of Christ's 'all-surpassing power' in action:

> Jack is an ex-miner, a big man. He was notorious in the area for being 'one of the lads', a very big drinker and a well-known womaniser. I can tell you, you would never believe that now: he is so transformed as to be almost unrecognisable.

Jack and his sister came to see me one day four years ago. They were obviously in something of a blind panic. I was going to take the funeral service of their mother, scheduled for a couple of days ahead. When I said how sorry I was she had died, Jack blurted out, 'She visited us last night!' What he told me was, in summary, this.

He and his sister, Mary, had been sitting together in the front room of their mother's house, where Mary also lived. Some time in mid-evening, Mary heard someone speaking upstairs. Her very young grandson was asleep upstairs at the time, so she poked her head round the door at the bottom of the stairs to see what it was all about. It was then, she claims, that she heard her mother calling to her. She was terrified and rushed back in to Jack. He said he would investigate. He went upstairs and into the first room he came to. He tells me that it was icy cold and he felt there was a presence there. He came down the stairs in one! Together Jack and Mary sat in the front room the night through, too petrified to do anything.

As soon as they could, the next morning they came to see me to ask me to do an 'exorcism', something I have never done before. A couple of days later, I went round to the house with two others and the minister of a neighbouring parish, and conducted an 'exorcism'. I spoke to Jack and Mary about the devil, about sin, about the Lord Jesus Christ. I read the story of Legion and then I prayed about the presence in the house and for Jack and Mary. Afterwards, before we left, Jack asked me if I thought it would be a good idea if he started reading the Bible and coming to church. I said they were both excellent ideas!

I did some Bible studies with Jack, and he started to come along to church. Soon he was born again. A couple of weeks ago, he said to a lady in church, 'You know, I'm four years old in August.'

Compare that story, which glorifies the power of Christ, with the following remark by a Christian advertising agent, who both represented the Coca-Cola Corporation and engineered the 'I Found it' evangelistic campaign. He said, 'Back in Jerusalem where the church started, God performed a miracle there on the day of Pentecost. They did not have the benefit of buttons and media, so God had to do a little supernatural work there. But today, with our technology, we have available to us the opportunity to create the same kind of interest in a secular society.' Thus we are shown a container for the gospel which is so brilliantly clever that we almost feel the treasure should be grateful to be held in such a wonderful jar!

This does not sound like Paul. Fragile, flawed, thoroughly human 'jars' can hold the priceless treasure of Christ. We carry him on behalf of the world.

> What is in us is greater than we are; thus the content is greater than the vessel. Whether the vessel cracks in the enterprise or merely overflows is a matter of indifference. Only one thing matters: the tidings we bear must go forward.
>
> *(Balthasar)*[1]

A thorn in the flesh

God gave Paul extraordinary blessings: he was 'caught up to paradise' (2 Cor 12:4). However, as a counterweight, 'to keep me from becoming conceited because of these surpassingly great revelations, there was given me a thorn in my flesh, a messenger of Satan, to torment me' (v 7). A 'thorn', literally a 'stake in the flesh', is a powerfully physical image, as if Paul felt himself transfixed, pinned down and humiliated by whatever his ailment was. This 'thorn' came from God, but it was 'a messenger of Satan', suggesting perhaps a person or a group who followed Paul around, subverting his ministry. Yet 'in my flesh' implies a physical condition, a disability of some kind, which painfully affected him at times. In his letter to the Galatians, Paul writes gratefully about the kindness and understanding he found there: 'Even though my illness was a trial to you, you did not treat me with contempt or scorn' (Gal 4:13–14). He could be referring to an unpleasant or repellent condition, or perhaps it was something quite simple but frustrating and, for a public speaker, embarrassing, like a stammer.

Thankfully, we are not told Paul's trouble: each of us can apply his words to our own circumstances, in the same way that each of us can probably tell of a 'thorn in the flesh' from which we have often prayed for deliverance without apparent response from God. Many preachers have their 'thorns'. The great George Whitfield noted in his journal that he almost dreaded times of blessing on his ministry, because he knew they would be followed by days of black depression. A prominent London preacher is subject to attacks of vomiting before a service when he is due to preach. And a lady in South Yorkshire writes:

> I've lived with pain and illness for a long time, and three years ago I nearly died. I was so ill, the doctor stopped all my medication, and I was left in agony and torment. I asked God to let me die, but the Lord said, 'No I don't want you to die – you haven't finished yet.'
>
> He gave me the will to live and, although I was still in intense pain, my little room was full of joy and peace. A nurse commented on the peaceful atmosphere in my room; even the matron said that if a nurse was missing, she always knew where to find her.
>
> Whenever I'm down, God always lifts me up and shows me a sign, sometimes through my readings. Once I was having communion and was really depressed, until I

put the bread in my mouth. Then God spoke to me and said, 'My grace is sufficient.' He really understands our human feelings, and his love will overlook our failings.

Sometimes my husband and boys are so spiritually full, we can sit for a long time full of happiness and peace; there is no need for words between us. I can't remember when the Lord first touched me, but I do know of his great love for me, and I know he'll never leave me.

The 'thorns' God gives us are there to keep us sane, and to save us from abusing his blessings and spiritual gifts by allowing them to feed our vanity. It does not do for us to get too attached to our gifts, in case we delude ourselves into thinking they are an intrinsic part of our personalities. Our 'thorns' keep us where we are at our best – close to the Lord and dependent on him for our usefulness. We may once have thought that divine power came to displace human weakness, but Paul teaches us another way. Human weakness and divine grace go hand in hand. God triumphs through what is least attractive about us. Our weaknesses serve to magnify God's grace and wisdom in a way mere human perfection could never do. The greater our weaknesses as God's servants, the more obvious is the power of his all-sufficient grace:

He said to me, 'My grace is sufficient for you, for my power is made perfect in weakness.' Therefore I will boast all the more gladly about my weaknesses, so that Christ's power may rest on me.

Chapter 14

TO KNOW THE FELLOWSHIP OF HIS SUFFERINGS

Clay jars and thorns are symbols of Christ's power coming to its fullness in our weaknesses. Conditions so negative as apparently to sabotage our Christian usefulness become the Lord's way into our gaping need. Such is the astounding grace of God. Our weaknesses and shortcomings, the pressure we are under, the spiritual hostilities we face, can all serve God's purpose, because they will either destroy us or turn us around, naked and desperate, to face the Lord.

And thus we 'know Christ'. The New Testament sense of 'knowing' is 'to recognise, feel, appropriate' (Lightfoot): a total knowing, like that of true friends who know each other through commitment, promise, faithfulness and moving on together. To know Christ in that way was Paul's driving passion. He needed more than correct theological ideas about Christ's place in the plan of salvation; he wanted to come close to the one 'who loved me and gave himself for me' (Gal 2:20):

I consider everything a loss compared to the surpassing greatness of knowing Christ Jesus my Lord ... I want to know Christ and the power of his resurrection and the fellowship of sharing in his sufferings, becoming like him in his death...

(Philippians 3:8,10)

Page after page in the four Gospels tell of Jesus' sufferings and trials, the cost to him of his love for us and for his Father in the face of sin and unbelief: the shallowness of the crowds, the hardness of the people of God, the dullness of friends, the failure of his disciples, the blind hypocrisy of a vindictive religious establishment, the barbarity of corrupt political power, his loneliness, his message mocked, his death on the cross ridiculed. He was indeed God's suffering servant.

However, merely listing Jesus' desolating experiences does not convey the true cost to him. Living in this world was, for him, like Mozart compelled to listen to his loveliest music played out of tune. We cannot begin to fathom the depth of his endurance. And yet we can, as it were, touch Christ in his sufferings by means of the sufferings we endure through being faithful to the Father. The astounding truth is that by our sufferings we join with Jesus and come to 'know the fellowship of sharing in [his] sufferings'.

It is not merely that we suffer on account of Jesus, but that we come into solidarity with him. As we respond to scripture and 'fix our eyes on Jesus ... who endured such opposition from sinful men' (Heb 12:2–3), our own experiential knowledge of the cost of discipleship resonates with his. It is as if the shared experience creates between Christ and his people a shared language of suffering.

> 'Remember the words I spoke to you: "No servant is greater than his master." If they persecuted me, they will persecute you also.'
>
> *(John 15:20)*

For many Christians down the ages and even today, to share with Christ in his sufferings has resulted in their paying the ultimate price. Yet their witness endures.

God's people seem at their best in martyrs' churches. The explanation, surely, is to do with the depth of 'knowing Christ ... in the fellowship of his sufferings', a knowing that is denied to those of us who are insulated from it by our easy-going relationship with the world.

Becoming like him in his death

The statues of ten modern Christian martyrs were unveiled recently on the west front of Westminster Abbey in London.

Wang Zhiming, a pastor, was executed in 1973 at a gathering of over 10,000 Chinese Christians, who were forced to witness his death in an official attempt to scare them into submitting to the Maoist system.

Lucian Tapiedi was a teacher and an evangelist in Papua New Guinea. He was hacked to death in 1942, during the Japanese invasion, by a man who later became a Christian.

Oscar Romero, Archbishop of San Salvador, was murdered in a hospital chapel in 1980. He was one of a succession of priests killed for espousing the cause of the poor and persecuted. His church documented human rights abuses in which people disappeared without a trace. He once said that murdered priests were 'testimony of a Church incarnated in the problems of its people'.

Martin Luther King, a Baptist minister, was shot dead in April 1968 at the age of 39, a year after he was awarded the Nobel Peace Prize for his civil rights campaign which transformed America.

Esther John was born an Indian Muslim. She attended a Christian school in Pakistan and was converted through reading Isaiah 53. She refused to marry a Muslim, and worked as an evangelist in the Punjab. Esther was found dead in her bed in February 1960, her skull smashed twice with a heavy, sharp instrument.

Police suggested it was the work of a disappointed lover. But after investigation, they reported, 'We have found no clue. This girl was in love only with Christ.'

Elizabeth of Russia, a martyr of the Orthodox Church, was murdered in July 1918. One of her Bolshevik killers, Ryabov, gave this account: 'After throwing her down the shaft, we heard her struggling for some time. Then I threw in a grenade. After a short while, we heard talking and a terrible groan. I threw another grenade. And what do you think – from beneath the ground we heard singing!' They ran out of grenades and filled the shaft with dry brushwood which they set alight. 'The hymns still rose up through the thick smoke for some time yet.'

Janani Luwum, Archbishop of Uganda, Rwanda, Burundi and Boga-Zaire, was taken away and murdered after protesting to Idi Amin about the violence of his security forces. He had said, 'They are going to kill me. I am not afraid.'

Dietrich Bonhoeffer was executed on the scaffold at the Flossenburg concentration camp in 1945, a month before VE Day. He was an outspoken opponent of the Nazi party, and prophesied as early as 1932 that 'we must not be surprised if also for our church there will be times when the blood of martyrs will be called for'.

Manche Masemola, of South Africa, was murdered by her own parents in February 1928, when she was 16. Her parents were animists, of the Pedi tribe, struggling to eke out an existence on barren reserved lands in the Transvaal, where converts to Christianity were viewed with suspicion. Manche, who was never photographed, was not sent to school, but worked with her family. She converted to Christianity after going to hear Father Augustine Moeka, known as 'the Apostle of Sekhukhuneland', preach at a mission set up by the Anglican Community of the Resurrection. She wanted to attend church classes, but was discouraged by her parents who sent her to the traditional initiation school. There she underwent a symbolic ritual circumcision. When she still insisted on being Christian, her parents began to administer beatings, out of fear that she would refuse to marry and have children. Manche is reported as saying, 'If they cut off my head, I will never leave the faith.' She predicted to Father Moeka, 'I shall be baptised with my own blood.' Her parents finally took her to an isolated place and, according to a witness, beat her to death. A few days later, her younger sister died and was buried beside her, by a granite rock on a hillside.

> The world was not worthy of them.
> *(Hebrews 11:38)*

According to the apostle Peter, the first churches were concerned not so much with escaping persecution and martyrdom in the struggle against the powers of darkness, but remaining faithful in the test:

> ...now for a little while you may have had to suffer grief in all kinds of trials. These have come so that your faith – of greater worth than gold, which perishes even though refined by fire – may be proved genuine and may result in praise, glory and honour when Jesus Christ is revealed.
> *(1 Peter 1:6–8)*

'...and the power of his resurrection'

It cuts both ways. By our experience of suffering as we pursue the will of God, we share in Christ's sufferings and he shares in ours. While Paul was still Saul and hounding the churches, the ascended Lord Jesus stopped him dead in his tracks with the question, 'Why do you persecute me?' (Acts 9:4–5). If Paul was about to reply that he had never laid a finger on Jesus personally, he was saved by the sudden realisation that Christ is one with his people and they are one with him. Touch one of them and you touch him; bless them and you bless him. Paul's great teaching on the church as the body of Christ (1 Cor 12) was born out of his experience on the Damascus Road.

Our lives participate in the full range of Christ's life. We are, we love to say, 'Easter people'. We are indeed, but only because we are first 'Good Friday people', in dynamic fellowship with everything Jesus endured for us. Our present lives track the contours of his life described in the Gospels, through suffering and darkness into resurrection life. We go that way because he went that way: 'For just as the sufferings of Christ flow over into our lives, so also through Christ our comfort overflows' (2 Cor 1:5). Those who are one with Christ must be prepared to drink his cup (Matt 20:22). If we wish to share in his glory, we must also be willing to share in his sufferings (Acts 14:22; Rom 8:17–18; 2 Tim 2:12). There is a two-thousand-year gap between Christ's earthly life and ours, between the price he paid for doing the Father's will and the price we pay now. Nevertheless, by our sufferings, such as they are, endured as his faithful people in a dark world, we know (recognise, feel, appropriate) Christ in his sufferings.

Knowing the fellowship of Christ's sufferings does not sit easily with our culture's prevailing obsession with 'the self'. How many sermons on Philippians 3:10 ('I want to know Christ and the power of his resurrection') have you heard, or preached, which have omitted the second part of the verse – 'the fellowship of sharing in his sufferings'? Our instinct is to divide the text into two quite different spiritualities: first, the 'power of Christ's resurrection', which seems to us thrilling, optimistic, full of glorious promise; and then the 'fellowship of his sufferings', which seems strange, forbidding and mystical. But Paul would have found such a separation inconceivable. Christ is one; his experience is one; and our union with him encompasses all that he received in his body.

Sufferings bring in the End

We naturally think that our witness would be more effective, certainly our lives would make smoother progress, without the added freight of these times of testing and hardship. But Paul had more to say concerning the trials he endured in his work of evangelism and church planting.

> Now I rejoice in what was suffered for you, and I fill up in my flesh what is still lacking in regard to Christ's afflictions, for the sake of his body, which is the church.
> *(Colossians 1:24)*

Paul is not here referring to Christ's passion. The idea of expiation and satisfaction for sins is wholly absent from this verse. The word translated 'afflictions' is nowhere in the New Testament applied to Jesus' death, which was 'the one full, perfect and sufficient sacrifice, oblation and satisfaction for the sins of the whole world'.

The Lord Jesus, the suffering servant, paid the price of his Father's love for the world in his own body. Now, since Pentecost, he is in the world as the 'corporate Christ', the Messianic community, the church, his body. He is bringing all creation home to the Father. And still there is a price to pay, sufferings to be borne, hostilities to be faced in the world. But it is through his people – his body, the church – that Christ suffers in the present age. What is now experienced by his people, their own personal trials and pain, 'fills up' or supplements his own earthly sufferings in the days of his incarnation.

Scripture speaks of the suffering that Christ's body, the church in the world, will endure in the present age: there will be a quota of sufferings, a story of costly faithfulness, for a fixed period of time (Matt 24:6; Mark 13:8; Luke 21:9,24). Similarly, Hebrews 11:40 suggests that the sufferings of God's faithful witnesses in former times need to be supplemented by those of the Christian church before the process is complete and the End comes. Scripture defines the amount of sin and wickedness, and the number of conversions, to be completed (Matt 23:32; Rom 11:25; 1 Thess 2:16), which implies that evangelism holds the key to the process. All this is known only to the Father and hidden from human intelligence.

Our earlier reflections on jars and thorns have emphasised the identification of Christ's experiences with our own. But Colossians 1:24 shows the clear distinction between his suffering then and our suffering now. In his incarnation, Jesus did everything required for the salvation of the world; but he left room for his people, since Pentecost, to contribute towards that measure of suffering known only to the Father. Thus our experiences, both public and secret, which are incurred because we are Christians, bring something to the story of Christ and his people in the world. This is a real 'filling up' of what Christ has left to us to do, a process which will never be completed until the church's conflict with sin and unbelief is brought to a close at the End.

And Paul is glad to be able to contribute his share to that totality of things suffered for Christ's sake (Acts 9:16). Any sufferings which a Christian endures as a Christian are contributed on behalf of the whole body (1 Cor 12:26) and go towards building up a stable, faithful Messianic community. The price of discipleship is not merely a necessary evil, an unfortunate by-product of faithfulness, but rather helps to complete the story and bring the End closer.

So to the tenth modern martyr whose statue was recently unveiled at the west front of Westminster Abbey. When **Maximilian Kolbe** returned to Poland from Japan in the 1930s, his prominent ministry inevitably attracted the attention of the Nazis. He was arrested and sent to Auschwitz concentration camp, where he gave his food away to other prisoners and defied the authorities by holding services. In August 1941, Kolbe was killed by lethal injection after he freely offered his life in place of a father of a family. The starvation cell where he died is now a shrine. Once again evil was outwitted by a Christian whose self-sacrificing love speeds the coming of the End.

Chapter 15

ORCHESTRATIONS

Syntonisation occurs when a note played on one instrument produces the corresponding note on another instrument placed near to it. The lesser energy repeats the rhythm of the greater energy in its own way: as when a child begins to dance and hum when she hears a favourite tune; or a stick thrown into a fast-flowing stream takes on the motion of the water; or a hovering kestrel will adjust its contours and movements in perfect response to the wind.

Liken God to a composer who conducts the orchestra as they play his music. Each musician plays in his or her own way. Each is released by the music and also held under its discipline. Each one plays and gives back to the composer his own music. God the composer, the higher energy, releases and orchestrates the lesser energies of our lives. We move under his direction, repeating his rhythms in our selves. His redeeming activity is not a fixed, unvarying constant, like gravity. He moves within and upon situations, bringing them to maturity, to a point of readiness, when they rise and surge to a peak of spiritual potential. Our own usefulness lies within the rhythms of the Spirit's activity, when we surrender our lives each day to God's timing in our affairs:

> O let thy sacred will
> All thy delight in me fulfil!
> Let me not think an action mine own way,
> But as thy love shall sway,
> Resigning up the rudder to thy skill.

This is George Herbert's prayer for syntonisation between the almighty Lord and our minuscule powers.[1]

The Greek New Testament has a word for God's timing which persuades people, events, things, needs and resources to intersect in a moment of blessing and transformation – kairos. People who are weak enough for God to use will find immense joy and encouragement in kairos. You put a saucepan of milk on a hot stove and wait while nothing happens. Then suddenly the milk surges up as it comes to the boil. In that moment, it does not matter what time is on the clock (chronos time); all the signs are that it is time to lift the saucepan off the stove now, at once, immediately (that is kairos time).

The story of Manna

> During the latter part of 1982, I was coming through a rather dark period in my life. I found it a frightening experience. Life had been fairly clear up till then. A passage from the Psalms ... 'O that you would listen to my voice, harden not your heart' ... broke into the darkness. Somehow that glimmer of light let me see and, in a strange way, feel the pain and injustice on the streets around me. I felt I was called to do something about it.

Thus Nanette Ffrench describes the kairos moment which led to the founding of the Manna Centre and its work among homeless people and refugees in London.[2] Church authorities gave her a disused nursery school, leaking roof, no electricity and no water.

> One of the first visitors was my brother, Barry. We lit a candle and prayed together. Local churches became interested and a frequent visitor, James (who spent his nights in the park as he was barred from a men's hostel), told me one morning that he knew where we could get bread for nothing. He introduced me to Pinto at the bakery in Bermondsey Street. For years we collected all the bread we needed, free of charge – surely manna from heaven!

Later Manna was given a property in Fulham, where they now offer temporary accommodation to single women who come to the UK from abroad seeking asylum. Nanette Ffrench writes:

> Our task, however, is more than just providing accommodation. Many come from their home country quite traumatised, and one of the needs is emotional support. For expert assistance, we frequently refer to the Medical Foundation who treat victims of torture. Other tasks are invariably required. To mention just a few examples: signing them up for income support; introducing them to doctors; helping them to find a solicitor, so that their appeal to the Home Office is done in a timely and competent manner; introducing them to local educational facilities, since many wish to learn or improve their English and/or other skills; it is important to help them get used to the transport system; and, last but not least, ensuring that all in the household get along with each other.
>
> As with our work in the Manna Centre, we see the provision of accommodation to the poor as a basic

human right and as a sign that the community is sharing responsibility for the proper use of the resources of the nation.

One of our former residents from the Philippines writes, 'Farm Lane has given pleasure and happiness to each individual who stops at the door, realising the warm welcome you give and discovering a place or a room to stay, however long or short that may be. Words can't express my feeling of gratitude, and I am really and sincerely grateful that I'm one of the few chosen to experience life in this so-called special home.'

A Christian woman home from her work abroad, back in London, unsure of the future and God's will for the next stage of her life endures 'a dark period ... a frightening experience'. Then there is an apparently fortuitous inter-secting of influences, individuals and events. God speaks to her out of scripture concerning local people in trouble. She becomes aware of the real need among the homeless. Light breaks in. God's directing call, the surprising provision of essential resources and advice from key individuals, all flow together under the persuasion of the Holy Spirit to give birth to a new ministry. Nanette Ffrench finds herself, in all her weakness, enmeshed in a kairos moment. The Lord, composer and conductor, changes the music and gives her a new part to play, delighted to receive back from her a fresh interpretation.

Kairos time

For believers in the biblical world, chronos time – that of the calendar and the clock – was of very little interest. What mattered was to be involved in God's kairos time, for that is when things happen. One day of God's kairos time is worth a thousand years of empty chronos time (Psalm 84:10). Kairos transforms the way we perceive our part in God's purposes. It means release from preoccupation with our own importance, our powers and abilities, within the divine plan.

> ...'Lord, what about him?'
> '...what is that to you? You must follow me.'
> *(John 21:21–22)*

Kairos shifts the centre of gravity away from ourselves and onto God. We can stop taking ourselves too seriously. The need to be successful can become an idol, absorbing our energies and devouring our humanity. But a sense of powerlessness may be the saving of us, persuading us to find our usefulness within the Spirit's rhythms. Kairos is why a relatively tiny number of people, after Pentecost, felt able to respond to the Lord's command to 'go and make disciples of all nations' (Matt 28:18-20). Kairos helps us to see what a contemplative was getting at when she said, 'The best way to care for the world is not to care.'

The *kairos* master-class

Central to the way Jesus prepared his disciples for their mission after Pentecost were his lessons in kairos encounters. He taught them to look, to gather all the relevant information possible and to interpret the present time (Luke 12:54–56). Just as fishermen and farmers can glance at the sky and forecast tomorrow's weather, so believers should expect to read and interpret what the Spirit is establishing. Indeed, Jesus makes the startling judgement that it is hypocritical for a believer to be smart at reading the signs when it comes to making a living but inept at discerning God's action in the world. There is no need for us to blunder around, crashing into locked doors. Instead, with a praying mind and sensitive spirit, we should seek the potentially fruitful kairos encounters, when the Spirit has left doors on the latch.

A classic kairos encounter takes place right at the beginning of Jesus' ministry, during the wedding at Cana:

> Jesus said to the servants, 'Fill the jars with water'; so they filled them to the brim.
>
> Then he told them, 'Now draw some out and take it to the master of the banquet.'
>
> They did so, and the master of the banquet tasted the water that had been turned into wine.
>
> *(John 2:7–9)*

We can imagine those servants panicking as they saw the original stock of wine dwindle away. Even Jesus' mother, Mary, had no idea what could be done to save the situation. But, in her powerlessness, she broke through to the secret of kairos, which is to 'do whatever he tells you' (v 5).

'Now' is the kairos word. Now the Lord has responded to human need. Now he has taken hold of inadequate resources, the jars of water, and worked a miracle of love, supplying the very best wine. Not ten seconds earlier, while the water was still only water, but now.

Peter Kimber, chief executive of Scripture Union England and Wales, provides another fascinating example of a kairos encounter:

> When I was Chairman of SU in Scotland, we were faced with a headquarters building in urgent need of repair. Everyone in evangelical circles knew of 280 St Vincent Street. It was an end-terrace house in the business district of central Glasgow, with a large garage at the rear. In many ways, however, it was not ideal. There was

no parking. There was no space for storing things like tents, canoes, dinghies and all the normal paraphernalia of camping. The value of the building was estimated at about £250,000.

It was a discouraging time, one which I remember chiefly for struggles about money and internal conflicts over how the movement should be funded. The delay in finding premises was depressing for everyone, I think, because the old building and the furniture in it cried out for renewal. Our prayer times on Council had a certain doggedness about them, without a lot of hope. Finding a new building exercised us for a couple of years, and we looked at scores of possibilities without success. We narrowed down our wish list to somewhere within the circle of the Glasgow underground railway, with good communications, parking for at least twenty cars, more office accommodation than we needed, to allow for expansion, and storage space for camping gear.

Eventually, and quite suddenly, a number of things changed. A large vacant site across the road from our existing building was purchased by Britoil, later to be bought over by British Petroleum. Consequently, our building doubled in value and we put it on the market at £500,000. We soon had a potential buyer.

At the same time, we heard rumours that a large manufacturing company was considering letting or selling their purpose-built premises. The company manufactures such well-known products as photographic film and tape for audio and video recording. Their building had two floors of office and meeting space, plus a large warehouse standing in its own grounds with parking for fifty cars, hard by the motorway and within the circle of the Glasgow underground. Graham Wilson, on the SU staff, first brought this building to our attention, adding, 'This building would be absolutely perfect for our purposes, but we could never afford it.'

We entered negotiations for purchasing the building and got to the day before papers had to be signed, when our General Director phoned me at work to say that the deal had fallen through. The company had had a better offer and owed it to their shareholders to get the best deal they could. I wrote to the Chairman, pointing out that he had a perfect right to get a better deal, but that we had a mission to the young people of Scotland and wondered if he would consider sticking with our bid. After an interesting few days, he wrote back to say that he had reconsidered the position and was happy to let us have the building at the original price.

To cut a long story short, we eventually sold 280 St Vincent Street for £475,000 and bought the other building for £350,000. The result was that we had a huge warehouse, large enough to contain all the tents, dinghies and canoes and equipment, which previously had been scattered in the garages and sheds of obliging supporters all over Glasgow. Maintenance could proceed during the winter, in civilised and heated surroundings.

But why was the building sold so quickly and cheaply? The reason emerged in a very strange way. My family at that time lived in a house in Edinburgh onto which we had built a flat for my father-in-law. About this time he remarried, and we let out that flat to a young woman. On Easter Sunday, we invited our tenant and her boyfriend to have lunch with us, in the course of which the boyfriend asked if I had something to do with SU. When I confirmed my interest, he said, 'Do you know why the company sold you that building so cheaply?'

'No, but I am extremely delighted that they did,' I replied.

He then explained that he was a cameraman for Scottish Television which bought much of their film from the company. Recently, they had cancelled all their orders, as had the BBC. The reason was that someone in the company had used the wrong kind of adhesive to hold a layer of plastic foam on the top and bottom of the large cans that hold the reels of video tape. Instead of a dry adhesive they had used a wet one which slowly seeped through the foam and onto the edge of the tapes. As the tapes passed over the recording heads in the video cameras, this adhesive was deposited on the heads, ruining them. They had to be replaced every six weeks or so at a cost of £20,000 and upwards. When the cause of the trouble was identified, the TV companies cancelled their orders, making the Glasgow business no longer viable, and work was concentrated in their distribution centre in England.

It is when I look back on the train of circumstances which gave rise to the purchase of our splendid building that I marvel at the way God works. Two crucial things had to happen before we could get the building that was so valuable. First, Britoil had to locate their HQ across the road from 280 St Vincent Street, thereby doubling the value of our office. Second, the company had to sell at a low price at just the right time. For this to happen someone had to make a mistake in applying an adhesive, making a lot of people very unhappy, but answering our prayers in a wonderful way.

There is an ironic sequel to this succession of events. The Britoil building was occupied for only a short time as BP, the late owners of it, relocated their activities. Subsequently, it was partly used by a building society. The SU building at 280 St Vincent Street was handsomely refurbished and let out as offices, but, I gather, has never been fully occupied since then.

The new SU building at Canal Street has been in full operation since day one. Part of the land surrounding it was sold for the building of a Christian resource centre, housing a number of other Christian movements. Most recently, a number of developers have been wanting to buy the site for a more profitable redevelopment, since it is a prime site for the purpose.

The lessons continue

Jesus continued to press home the principle of kairos throughout his ministry, through his teaching and his miracles. He demonstrated his mastery of timing when he called his first disciples (Luke 5:1–11). Even before they knew him, they were enmeshed in a kairos encounter that fixed in their minds the way the Lord works in the world. To those tired and disappointed fishermen, he said, 'Put out into deep water, and let down the nets for a catch' (v 4) – not here, or there, but in that spot over there. Jesus knew where the fish were now and where they would be in five minutes' time.

His invitation to them to follow him was based on that lesson in kairos: 'Don't be afraid' of the magnitude and complexity of the task and their limited abilities; 'from now on you will catch men' (v 10) – not because of their astounding powers of communication, but because their Lord is able to penetrate the world hidden below the surface of human thought and behaviour.

Jesus repeated that practical demonstration after his resurrection (John 21:1–14). To his confused, shame-faced, failed disciples, he reiterated the same principle: their impotence, his wisdom and power; their obedience, the promised catch. 'Throw your net on the right side of the boat and you will find some' (v 6).

We have our part to play. We can look after the boat, maintain the nets and establish the fishing enterprise. But surely we are not required to shoulder burdens that are not ours to carry but the Master's. A church nervy and anxious, depressed by mission, is not living in the freedom and joy of the kairos principle. No need for panic or despair, whatever the task and however limited our resources and abilities. Look, listen, interpret, go prayerfully into each day. And if the orchestration is the Lord's, then the results are his doing also.

Kairos beyond Pentecost

The kairos principle, dimly understood by the disciples before Jesus' death, came to life for them at Pentecost, with the advent of the Holy Spirit to 'teach you all things and ... remind you of everything I have said to you' (John 14:26). We see how the risen Lord came back to his people in the Holy Spirit, to walk ahead of them, orchestrating kairos encounters as he had done during his mission on earth. The crisis of the first persecution following Stephen's martyrdom (Acts 8:1–4) resulted in Christian dispersion (expansion!) into 'Phoenicia, Cyprus and Antioch' (11:19–21). And, as a direct consequence of this, Paul's great centre of missionary outreach was established.

Philip was willing to be directed by the Spirit to leave his flourishing ministry in Samaria, and to go and wait by 'the desert road – that goes down from Jerusalem to Gaza' (8:26–39). While God was moving his servant into position with one hand, with the other hand he was manoeuvring an Ethiopian official towards a kairos encounter. Somebody had sold the Ethiopian the copy of Isaiah he was reading at the time. A mechanic had serviced his chariot so that it safely reached that spot for that moment. Everything surged to the point of readiness, and Philip was there, waiting to step in and lead the man to faith in Christ.

Peter received his vision on a roof top in Joppa (Acts 10:9–23) even while the Lord was guiding Cornelius' men along the road from Caesarea, fifty miles away. As Peter was pondering the meaning of his vision, his answer was knocking at his front door. Thus Peter was able to break out of the confines of Judaism and share the gospel with a seeking Gentile centurion.

Kairos moments do not stand still. They rise, they peak and fall away.

For a time, in the early years of a remarkable outreach to international students in Cambridge, the largest single ethnic group attending the friendship and faith-sharing events were Iranian. Lovely, liberal, friendly, open-minded young men and women were coming in large numbers to Cambridge for various courses, but mostly to learn English. Then came the Ayatollah's revolution in Iran and, as if by magic, those young Iranians disappeared virtually overnight. One moment they were there, free to engage with the gospel; the next they were gone and, as far as we could tell, so was their contact with the Christian faith. The leaders of the work in Cambridge were deeply affected by this event. They decided that, from then on, they should act according to kairos and seize the moment filled with divine activity. They also decided that they would call their ministry 'Kairos'.

The great majority of the Christian churches in Cambridge carried on as if nothing had happened. There seemed to be no awareness of the timing of those events, of God's timing and of our duty as kairos people to be agile enough to respond to unique encounters orchestrated by the Holy Spirit. The churches were busy with their round-the-year programmes, quite unable, it seemed, to look beyond and 'interpret the present time', even though their television screens were full of images of Islamic fundamentalists making life impossible for Christians witnessing in Iran. The Iranian opportunity appeared suddenly in Cambridge, stayed a short while and disappeared. That is the nature of kairos.

Close encounter in Bradford

Seldom are we given unambiguous advance notice. More usually, awareness that we are involved in an orchestration of the Spirit dawns upon us only as we move into the encounter – or not even then, but much later, as we reflect on events.

If I may illustrate this truth from a personal experience: home from Thailand permanently, I was busy trying to interest young people in the opportunities for work in East Asia. On one occasion I went to Bradford, where we had meetings with school and church groups in the public library. One adult visitor sat through the day's events, observing and listening. At the end of the day, he came up and introduced himself as a Christian and a serviceman on leave from Germany. He said that God had spoken to him that day, directing him towards the possibility of missionary service. I wished him well and, I have to say, hardly gave the incident another thought, although I did hear later that he had entered theological college.

A number of years later, my wife and I had the opportunity to return to Thailand for a visit. While there, we attended a conference for believers in Thai churches. The conference was chaired by an impressive Thai who, we discovered, was head of the main school in the tough notorious border town where we had worked years earlier. He astonished us with the news that the church in that town now numbered seventy people, which is staggering for Thailand and even more so in the south of the country. In our day, a rather feeble group of a dozen or so people would attend a service on Sundays.

Excited by this news, I asked how this had come about. He said it had begun while his teenage son was attending English language classes with a young Englishman, a missionary, who had recently moved to the town. Our head-teacher friend was so impressed by the kindness, and particularly the courtesy, of the missionary that he felt he ought to show his appreciation by attending the Christian instruction group. In that way he came to Christ, witnessed to others, and so the church grew in numbers and strength.

And who was that effective young missionary? My chance visitor in the Bradford library on that day years before! For a split second the curtain was drawn back and I glimpsed the Lord bringing things, circumstances and people to intersect for that moment of transformation. Suddenly, the apparent pointlessness of our enforced return took on a new significance. A man happened to be home on leave from Germany, and happened to hear of a meeting which coincided with the way his interests were moving. Our paths crossed in an apparently chance way. The encounter triggered a response, with the result that he went around the world to the very place we had left because of ill health. There he was used by God in ways far exceeding anything we had experienced!

The effect of that disclosure upon me was praise. The Lord is way ahead of us, working to bring us, in our weakness and our sense of inadequacy, into encounters with people, who encounter yet others, who encounter yet still more people, all within the Spirit's concealed orchestrations. Thus God's purposes are fulfilled.

> In the same way that God's presence can be anywhere and anytime, so too any act may be historic. One vote can change the result of an election, a joke at the right moment can change the course of a meeting, anywhere and anytime the most otherwise trivial gesture can and does have world-historic consequences. But we rarely realise the effect until too late. It is incumbent upon us to remember that each moment can be decisive and therefore historic.
>
> *(Lawrence Kushner)*[3]

Chapter 16

FINALLY YOURSELF

The previous chapter has left us with unfinished business. Ideas like syntonisation and the truth of kairos may help us to understand the sympathetic resonance between God's power and our powerlessness. But there remains 'the self', that mysterious, elusive something I call Myself, lurking around life's corners, murmuring darkly, 'Weak enough for God to use? Your weaknesses are not only out there, external to you, in tough circumstances and dark experiences; they are also, chiefly, in here. I am your powerlessness. As long as you have me, you will carry your impotence around with you.'

Well-meaning people tell us, 'Just be yourself', as if it is clear what this is. We can appreciate what they are trying to say and, of course, they are right. They want us to live by the fundamental integrity of being true to who we are, with no play-acting, neither underselling or overselling ourselves. They want to spare us the stress of trying to be someone we are not. Somehow everyone seems to know by instinct that there is a truth about the self with which we must harmonise.

Many go searching for their elusive self, sinking a shaft deep into their psyche, looking for the one who is looking. After years of study and meditation, a Zen monk arrived at what he believed was the final question, 'Who am I?' However, he was startled to hear a voice inside him reply, 'Who is asking?'

Many speak of the self as the enemy within which keeps us from happiness. In his poem 'Self-Slaved', Patrick Kavanagh decides that enough is enough: 'Me I will throw away'. If only.

In his grim little summary of scripture and universal personal experience, John Donne considers the perverse, self-destructive energies of the self:

> Nothing but man of all unvenomed things
> Doth work upon itself with inborn stings.

Today it is all very different from Donne's time, when lynx-eyed piety kept a close watch on the activities of the self, not trusting it an inch. Today the self reigns supreme. Self-worship has no doubt always been the essence of sin, but no other age has justified narcissism so enthusiastically; no other culture has so bluntly rejected self-denial as a means to spiritual health; we embrace instead the celebration of the self as the highest good. But this celebration goes hand in hand with a deep cynicism about the self. We need to come to a decision about the status of the self in relation to God's purposes.

Yourself: the first gift received

In the Genesis account of creation, God first called each part into existence and declared each to be 'good', meaning 'You are just what I intended you to be and I am delighted with you'. In being true to itself and to its Creator, each detail of the created order, from atoms to galaxies, is released to play its part in the higher drama of God's cosmic plan. Therefore 'the morning stars sang together and all the angels shouted for joy' (Job 38:7) as they were let into the fundamental secret of real existence, that we are most completely ourselves when we enter the

Lord's purposes for us. We cannot enter properly into God's plan unless and until we are ourselves. Thus the paradox, that God's service is perfect freedom, was imprinted on the texture of creation from the first.

> It is through giving us the power and courage to be ourselves, that God fulfils his purposes in us ... and the quest for The Self God has meant each of us to be is like the quest for happiness (which is indeed much the same thing) – it is not found by looking for it. We do not ask of God, 'What sort of person did you mean me to be?' – we say to him, 'Lord, what will you have me to do?'
>
> *(Farrer)*[1]

Doing the will of another and, at the same time, coming mostly deeply to oneself is beautifully suggested in that remarkable saying of Theresa of Lisieux: 'The good God always lets me long for what he wants to give me'.

People who are weak enough for God to use will be wise enough to accept the self he has designed for them. Our real usefulness begins the moment we see our existence as a gift: 'Everything is gift. The receiver of the gift is himself the first gift received.' The Father has bestowed on each one a self which is priceless, unique and mysterious (in the image of God), which stands half way between heaven and earth, able to receive and enjoy God himself: 'Lord, how could you give yourself to me, if you had not first given me to myself?' (Nicholas of Cusa).

But the self must be redeemed back into communion with God: 'The heart is deceitful above all things and beyond cure. Who can understand it?' (Jer 17:9). The self is bent, defaced, infected by the contagion of fallen human nature. It must be cleansed in the blood of Christ, born again in the Holy Spirit, reconciled to the Father and received into his family by adoption. It must be constantly exercised in holiness and love, until the image of the Son and the will of the Father are formed in it. But, and this is the point, it is still 'Myself', exactly this self given me from the beginning and none other. My redemption does not require my reinvention. And when, at the end of the journey, we have overcome by the power of God's grace and receive 'a white stone with a new name written on it, known only to him who receives it' (Rev 2:17), it will be this same continuous self, this original gift, which will become the new name.

Love for the self

When Jesus healed people, he was restoring to each of them his or her self. When he encountered Legion, the man with multiple demonic possession (Mark 5:1–17), he took hold of that shattered, atomised personality (v 9), torn apart as its hundred centres competed for control, and reclaimed, restored, repossessed and reintegrated it into one harmonious self, moving around one centre, 'sitting there, dressed and in his right mind' (v 15). In place of his crazed behaviour in the graveyard (vs 3–5), where his energies flew in all directions, he was now returned to himself in lovely syntonisation with the Lord Jesus, quiet, calm, alert, purposeful, ready to serve (vs 18–20), completely normal, even ordinary – his own mother would recognise him as her son. In being returned to his God-intended, Christ-restored self, the man could play his unique part in the Lord's plans.

Christ restores the self to people, enabling them to live free from either self-loathing or self-worship. One young woman describes the experience of receiving back from the Lord a new self-respect:

I suppose I've always believed that there was something outside of this world and that I'm susceptible to spiritual things. I've been able to sense evil and have memories of being awakened in the night, terrified by evil presences, and the Lord's prayer being the only thing I knew to say to drive them away.

I'd always been a very insecure person and never sure of my own acceptability. Six years ago, by the world's standards, it would have appeared that I had a lot going for me. And yet I never really knew how to give or accept love. I was hanging onto materialism and a shallow relationship for security and, at the same time, worrying about how safe my material standards were and whether I'd be able to maintain them.

Eventually I came to a point where I needed to make a decision involving my job, but couldn't make the decision for myself. I was too fearful about doing the wrong thing, so instead I walked straight into the enemy's trap. I went to see a clairvoyant, despite something inside me saying it was wrong...

Disturbed by this encounter, she made contact with a local church and came to a personal faith in Christ. But a sense of residual occult activity continued to trouble her. She writes:

Over the next few weeks, God explained to me that he was working deeply in my life and that I needed a 'clean environment' for him to work on. It was then that I began to realise just how many of my acquaintances were involved in the occult. I made a decision to sever a lot of old contacts, at least for the time being. For a while I was very lonely, but over the past couple of years the Lord has revealed to me the reasons for my fears and behaviour patterns. While he has been healing me, he's given me the kind of deep friendships I'd never known before. He's helped me to accept myself, and to receive and give the

love which makes life so worthwhile. I now have the
knowledge that our only real security lies in him.

There is such a thing as proper self-love, love for the self
God has given us to be. Jesus assumed this when he
asked that we extend it to include our neighbour (Matt
19:19). With the psalmist, we view the self as God's
dwelling place, a place worthy of our awe and respect: 'I
praise you because I am fearfully and wonderfully made'
(Ps 139:14). In the prevailing climate of self-centredness
and narcissism, it is difficult to mention self-love without
misunderstanding. Here is a definition: A proper self-love
requires that we seek the true good of the self; and not
the self as the true good.

'Seek the true good of the self'

'The world is full of Christian ideas gone mad'
(Chesterton). Selfhood is one such idea. To give you a
measure of the rampant self-centredness of our culture,
there are currently over seven hundred books in print in
the US whose titles contain the word 'self' – self-esteem,
self-realisation, self-fulfilment. We glimpse a culture
absorbed in itself. It is a form of lunacy, yet it derives
from the biblical revelation of self-worth, the self
designed and created by God and bestowed on each of us
as his first gift. We are responsible to God for the way we
cultivate the self.

What is the 'true good' of the self which will fit us to fulfil our role in God's purposes? At this point it may be help-
ful to step outside oneself and to look at the question
through the lens of Jesus' words, 'Do to others as you would
have them do to you' (Luke 6:31). I know that I would like
people to do all kinds of pleasing and flattering things for
me; but I also realise that those things have little to do with
'the true good of the self'. Good is done to me, I feel, when

I meet people who are growing, changing, reaching out into new territory as they travel deeper into God; people who think and read outside their comfort zone; who reject spiritual and intellectual junk food, lazy opinions, pre-packaged off-the-shelf views and clichéd banalities which too often pass between us as conversation.

I am challenged and inspired by such people. I find them disturbing. They cause me to think that 'the true good of the self' requires that I stop marching with the lemmings and do, instead, the hard work of seeking the life God has set me to live. And Jesus requires that I owe it, in love, to the people around me to be for them what my inspiring, disturbing friends are to me: to care enough for my neighbour to suggest that he or she abandon lemmingdom and seek authentic selfhood.

Here is another account of Christians whose example challenges me, the Sisters of Charity nursing the poor during the plague in France:[2]

> Their praying and living surely banished unreality as effectively as it can be banished in this life. There was no humbug about God. Their God was the love which controlled them, and whom they obeyed. They knew him as a horse knows its rider, by the hand on the reins. There was no humbug about themselves either; for they were wholly occupied in doing what they knew they must do; and they became what their God-given lives made of them. They had no time for studying their personalities in any mental looking-glass: they saw themselves only in the eyes of the poor, and in the eyes of their God.

'In the burl of being'

We must correct any misunderstanding arising from the story of Legion referred to earlier. This story illustrates the way Jesus restores disordered lives. But if we have an ounce of self-knowledge, we will be aware that the struggle continues long after all 'exorcisms' are over and done with! In our so-called 'normal' selves, we come up against the grain and texture of who we are. In a vivid phrase, poet Gerard Manley Hopkins spoke of God working with the 'burl of being'. A burl is a knot in a piece of wood, or a tight, tangled mass in wool.

To a chess player it makes little difference what the pieces on the board are made of: wood, ivory, plastic, glass, metal – his strategy and moves are not affected. But God is not a chess player and we are not his chess pieces. As the world population heads towards seven billion, it is essential to our witness that we hold to the astounding way he honours the distinctive self of each individual, not as a chess player, more like a woodcarver.

I have on the shelf in front of me a small, wooden owl carved in a rather abstract design. What still astonishes me, after many years of looking at it, is the way the carver has used the burl, the grain and the tone of the wood, which was a piece taken out of a hedge near Cambridge. The layers of feathers are suggested by the changing natural colour in the original wood. But it is the face and especially the eyes which use the natural textures so brilliantly. The grain swirls to the left and to the right of the beak to give the eyes of the owl. I ask myself how on earth did the artist know what was waiting for him inside this original, ordinary, rough piece of wood from the fens? How did he predict the swirl of the grain, the tint, the burl, and sense that it 'contained' a beautiful little owl? I guess it was by the wisdom acquired through years of experience handling and observing wood, touch and observation, previous successes and failures with the knife; the skill to unlock the inner life of the wood and to imagine the potential within, the small creature at its centre, waiting to be released.

As I look at my owl, it glows and breathes in a way machine-generated objects never do. They may be precise, flawless and endlessly replicated, but they do not have that quality D H Lawrence described:[3]

> Things men have made with wakened hands, and put soft life into are awake through years with transferred touch, and go on glowing for long years...

God is the woodcarver, working with the potential and limitations of the wood, accepting the challenge of each piece and bending his skills to suit it. He follows the nature of the wood, allowing its qualities and characteristics to lead the knife. Luther said of Jesus, 'He can ride the lame horse; he knows how to carve the rotten wood.'

Rotten wood flakes away at the slightest touch of the knife. But the knot, the burl, is a different proposition. It both spoils the wood and yet gives it its individuality and distinctive character. It is hard, awkward, stubborn, jutting out with its own kind of intense, tightly packed grain and rich, beautiful colour. The burl resists the carver's tools. As a metaphor of ourselves, 'the burl of being' is a hard, tight-grained concentration of personality, characteristics, quirky and off-centre, which gives us our individuality, for better or for worse.

God's love and power are evident as much in his adapting to the burl of our individuality as in his saving us from it. This he did for the human race when, in Jesus Christ, he shaped himself to our condition, and this he does for each of us individually. He wants us to be, for our sakes, not his. He will certainly take us with him into his mission but, as it were, indirectly and because we are, first, ourselves.

Original and individual

My little owl is a one-off: it is original and individual. And this is the romance of our life with God: he is forming us as originals and individuals. (Does that seem true of the Christians you know?) This is not about individualism, for individualism begins life as individuality but snatches it from God's hand and makes of it a kind of self-pleasing that is set over against other people. The consequences of such spiritual anarchy are evident all around us. 'I celebrate myself, and sing myself,' said Walt Whitman, but that enchanting vision has transpired to be a 'hollowness filled with nothing wrapped up in emptiness'.

So much for the fallacy of individualism. But individuality is God's special work. He sees already the owl waiting for release. He brings out the living, true distinctiveness of each.

Take as an example a man who had life-long trouble with the 'burl of his being', Jacob. His name tells all (Gen 25:26) and very unattractive it is: 'deceiver' and 'supplanter', lurking behind his brother from the moment of birth to outwit him. Jacob lived out his mother's dreams, or simply did what she told him: he tricked his brother, his father and his brother-in-law into giving him what he wanted. Watch your back when Jacob is around.

God came to Jacob in a way he would understand and at a level of power he could cope with, in the form of a man (32:22–32). All his life Jacob had struggled and schemed to come out on top. Now he would need to draw on all his resources – his pride, tenacity, intelligence and strength – as he wrestled with that mysterious stranger through the night, in the shallows of the Jabbok brook. But Jacob was wrestling with God, and God was working on Jacob, drawing on his knowledge of the man's nature. He knew the grain and the burl. The outcome? The opposite and discordant qualities which were Jacob became reconciled. He won, yet he was defeated. 'He struggled with the angel [messenger] and overcame him' is the language of power and success; 'he wept and begged for his favour' is the language of humility and need (Hosea 12:4). Jacob received a new name, Israel, and a born-again new beginning. But he walked away from that encounter with a limp. The shaping touch of the artist would live on in him all his life.

We can call Jacob an original not because he deliberately set out to make himself different (individualism) but because, in embracing God and begging for his blessing, his self breathed and thrived. He was probably not a smooth man, a well-adjusted man or a pleasing sort of man – he was a limping man in many ways – but he at last accepted the self God had given him. And Christians are Jacob's spiritual children.

Selving

Let us come back to the point we have been stressing all along: what we are is the service we render to God. Or, at least, we are unable to serve God as he desires until we are ourselves. Close the gap between being and doing. I am what I do if what I do is true to who I am.

Following this principle may cause us to slow down and deal with fewer people, but it will be at a more profound level. More of our time and attention will be engaged in observing the self in others. Jesus spent what may seem to us a disproportionate amount of time with individuals. He searched for the grain and the burl in each one. He honoured their individuality and gave them the respect each one deserved (see John 4:1–26). He looked 'hard' at things and at people for what Hopkins called their 'inscape' (landscape, seascape, why not inscape?): 'inscape is not a superficial appearance; rather it is the expression of the inner core of individuality, perceived in moments of insight by an onlooker who is in full harmony with the being he is observing' (Hopkins). Jesus looked for the inscape of people and of events (at Cana, for example) and fashioned his approach accordingly. It is a way of looking and sensing which the Holy Spirit will help us to cultivate.

To recognise the inscape of a person or object is to know what is essential and individual about them; not so as to control and manipulate them (a controlling, manipulative mind shuts itself off automatically from seeing inscape) but to honour them with a proper respect for the truth of their individuality. It is therefore a first step in seeking the true good of the person's self. The way God engaged with Jacob by the Jabbok is a striking example of an action appropriate to a person's distinctive inscape.

We will need real discernment to apply this principle in our own affairs. Raymond Fung tells of a lay evangelist friend in South India, who worked in an impoverished parish next to a huge slum:[4]

For years she worked among the poor, preaching and serving, refusing offers of greener pastures. But not many showed any clear inclinations towards the Christian way. One night, during a meeting with a group of girls who had fled their homes because of their fear of being sold into prostitution, she burst out in anger. Frustrated by the slave-like mentality of the girls who, given the terrible sufferings they had been subjected to, ought to know better, she found herself shouting at them: 'the one thing that will liberate you from bondage is the Gospel. To it you have shown no response. What can I say?' She threw up her hands, the room was silent. Then a girl timidly put up her hand and said: 'You have been so patient and so good to us, we thought we could never hope to be like you. We can never be good enough to be Christians.'

'My friend', says Fung, 'was shocked. But that evening proved to be a turning point in her ministry and in the lives of many of those girls!' We can guess that the evangelist looked in a new way for 'the inner core of individuality', the inscape, of those girls.

One of Hopkins' best poems may help us look for someone's inscape, what Hopkins also called 'selving':[5]

As kingfishers catch fire, dragonflies draw flame;
   As tumbled over rim in roundy wells
   Stones ring; like each tucked string tells, each hung bell's
Bow swung finds tongue to fling out broad its name;
Each mortal thing does one thing and the same:
   Deals out that being indoors each one dwells;
   Selves – goes itself; *myself* it speaks and spells;
Crying *What I do is me; for that I came.*

Everything in nature comes with its signature tune, its autograph, its distinct individuated 'selving'. The kingfisher on the wing does not set out to create an impression of fire flashing by. The dragonfly does not strive to look like a jet of flame from a blowpipe. Both are unmistakably themselves in doing what they do. This is their 'kingfisherness' and 'dragonflyness'.

Even pebbles have their individuality: no two stones sound the same when dropped from the same height into the same well. Creation is like an orchestra of many instruments, 'each tucked [plucked] string tells' as it vibrates at the pitch to which it has been set. Every sound does not blur into one great undifferentiated noise. Each bell is tuned to an exact set of harmonics by the bell-maker and matched to the others in the set. When struck by the 'tongue', it 'flings out' its name. What you hear is what it is.

What each thing does by its appearance, colour or

sound reveals its particular being which is hidden from our sight, 'indoors'. We know a thing not by its essence, but by the way we perceive it as it 'selves' (ie tells itself). What you hear, see or feel is what it is. What it is is what you get: 'myself it speaks and spells'. Thus each part of the created order contributes to the whole glorious hymn offered up in praise to God. It is the ministry of each part, however humble (kingfisher, dragonfly, pebble), to play its part in the symphony: 'Crying What I do is me; for that I came'.

Thus nature shows us what we are here for, what is the purpose of our existence, work and ministry. Each of us can say, 'What I do is me: for that I came.' But in nature it is all external; its outwardness is its 'selving' and its inscape. With us it is more than simple self-expression. We are created and redeemed to reflect back to God the image of his Son. Therefore our inscape and our selving arise out of our life in Christ. And so to the second verse of Hopkins' poem:

I say more: the just man justices;
    Keeps grace: that keeps all his goings graces;
Acts in God's eye what in God's eye he is -
    Christ. For Christ plays in ten thousand places,
Lovely in limbs and lovely in eyes not his
    To the Father through the features of men's faces.

The man in Christ does what he is. Justified by Christ, he will act with Christlike justice or goodness. If he keeps to the grace given him in Christ, all of the Christian's behaviour, 'his goings', will be touched by grace, gracious, pleasing God. He lives Christ, he 'selves' Christ, for Christ is with him and covers him. The believer's entire existence is mediated through Christ.

Christ has no body now on earth but yours. Yours are the
eyes through which his compassion must look out on the
world. Yours are the feet with which he must go about
doing good. Yours are the hands through which he must
bless the world now.

(Catherine of Sienna)

The final three lines of Hopkins poem bring to a profoundly satisfying climax everything we have said about
the self and selving, our inscape and our work, our powerlessness covered by Christ's power. 'Christ plays in ten
thousand places' like a wonderful singer singing a duet
with a frightened child. When we find ourselves inadequate, nervous, bumbling, amateur, caught in the spot-
light, frozen centre-stage, our lines forgotten, he steps in
like a brilliant actor and rescues the scene for us. This is
'Christ playing at me and me playing at Christ, only that
is no play but the truth' (Hopkins).

Hudson Taylor started us off on this exploration of
spiritual effectiveness. Tasked with evangelising inland
China, he discovered that the secret of blessing and
growth lay in the Christian's utter dependence on God, a
relationship he referred to as being 'weak enough for
God to use'. Our own circumstances are, of course, very
different from Hudson Taylor's, but the challenge is no
less daunting. We are living in a time of such tremendous and complex change that most of what we are now
doing as mission on behalf of the church will probably
not work for much longer. No one can tell us what the
emerging situation will be like. It also seems that in the
churches we are suffering from a kind of despair borne
of terminal self-reliance. This is a worrying prospect –
exhausted Christians faced with the demands of a society in fast transition. What are we to do? We can pack our
bags and move back to a more biblical spirituality of

fruitfulness, in which power comes to those who are wise enough to be 'weak enough for God to use'.